FIC   Arjouni, Jakob.

           And still drink
           more!

$16.95

DATE			

D1379828

MAR   1996

BAKER & TAYLOR

DRINK MORE!

A Kayankaya Mystery

Translated from the German by Anselm Hollo

NEW YORK
FROMM INTERNATIONAL
PUBLISHING CORPORATION

Copyright © 1987 Diogenes Verlag AG Zurich
Originally published as *Mehr Beir*

Translation copyright © 1994
Fromm International Publishing Corporation
560 Lexington Avenue
New York, New York 10022

Designed by C. Linda Dingler

Manufactured in the United States of America
Printed on acid-free recycled paper

First English edition 1994

Library of Congress Cataloging-in-Publication Data

Arjouni, Jakob.
  [Mehr Bier. English]
  And still drink more! : a Kayankaya mystery / Jakob Arjouni :
translated from the German by Anselm Hollo.– 1st English ed.
      p.   cm.
  ISBN 0-88064-161-4 (cloth : alk. paper) : $16.95
  I. Hollo, Anselm. II. Title.
PT2661.R45M4413   1994
833'.914–dc20   94-32004
                                                          CIP

5 4 3 2 1

April 1986

RHEIN MAIN FARBEN TO OPEN PLANT IN VOGELSBERG

TWO HUNDRED THOUSAND DEMONSTRATORS
EXPECTED IN VOGELSBERG

May 1986

POISON GAS SCANDAL

According to today's edition of *Le Monde*, the German concern *Rhein Main Farben* has sold basic ingredients for the manufacture of mustard gas to Iraq.

DUTCH SHIPOWNER BLOWS WHISTLE

Mr. Zoetemelk, a Dutch shipowner, has confirmed to journalists that his firm shipped several hundred barrels of chemicals produced by *Rhein Main Farben* to Iraq. He claims to have had no knowledge of the contents of these barrels. A spokesman for *Rhein Main Farben* disclaims any wrongdoing on the factory's part: "We were told the chemicals would be used purely for civilian purposes."

DEMONSTRATORS OCCUPY PLANT SITE

RHEIN MAIN FARBEN COMPLIES
WITH HESSE GOVERNMENT'S REQUEST
TO HALT PRODUCTION UNTIL FURTHER NOTICE

MAYOR OF FRANKFURT
ON RHEIN MAIN FARBEN PAYROLL
AS LEGAL CONSULTANT

June 1986

GREEN TERROR!
CHEMICALS MANUFACTURER MURDERED!

DEATH OF A GREAT MAN

"Friedrich Böllig was not only an outstanding comrade-in-arms
in the struggle for a clean future. He was a friend. All who knew
him will remember his consideration, kindness, and fairness. As
the head of one of the last family-owned concerns in our field,
he worked indefatigably for the development of new remedies,
particularly those used in the treatment of childhood diseases.
Friedrich Böllig's premature and tragic death is cause for uni-
versal grief."

FRANKFURT MAYOR'S WIFE
CONFIRMS SHE IS
RHEIN MAIN FARBEN SHAREHOLDER

DOES "RED ARMY FACTION" HAVE
"GREEN" SUCCESSOR?

RHEIN MAIN FARBEN
URGES PROMPT DECISION

Maximilian Funke, President of the Board of Directors: "If the
Hesse Government does not grant us a permit for our projected
plant in Vogelsberg, we must assume that the murderers of

Friedrich Böllig acted in the spirit of that government. It would make me very happy if such a suspicion proved unfounded."

November 1986

NO INCIDENTS
AT LAYING OF FOUNDATION STONE
OF RHEIN MAIN FARBEN PLANT IN VOGELSBERG

FORMER MAYOR OF FRANKFURT
APPOINTED PRESIDENT
OF UNITED NATIONS ENVIRONMENTAL
SECURITY COUNCIL

▪ DAY ONE ▪

▪1▪

The coffee was weak and the soft, moist cheese sandwich must have spent many days in the refrigerator. I tore chunks off it and washed them down with coffee. The sticky counter smelled of beer. Two meters to one side, a rumpled man dozed over his corn schnapps. From time to time he blew his nose, then wiped his mouth and forehead with the same handkerchief. He was staring at the framed verses above the sink: A FEW BEERS A NIGHT, THAT'S QUITE ALL RIGHT—A SCHNAPPS AT DAWN, YOUR HANGOVER'S GONE. I glanced at the sports pages next to his elbow

"How did Gladbach do?"

"Lost, two to zero," he mumbled, without raising his eyes.

I rapped on the counter.

"More coffee. A little stronger."

The proprietress pushed through the brown bead curtain, took my cup away, and brought it back with a refill. Her ample bosom was swathed in a ball gown from which her arms, neck, and head protruded like sausages. Her rear was adorned with a purple satin bow, her wrists with fake gold bracelets. Her hair had been dipped in liquid silver. Hertha was the owner of Hertha's Corner—open twenty-four hours. The place was large, dark, and empty. The dusty bottles behind the bar were lit up by fluorescence. Raindrops rattled against the dirty windowpanes. In one corner stood the table reserved for regulars, with its wrought-iron emblem, a wild sow waving a beer stein. Hertha was rinsing glasses. A fly landed on my mutilated sandwich. I lit a cigarette and blew smoke rings around the fly.

Time passes slowly in these early morning hours. It was eight thirty. My court date was at nine. I went to the john. The latch was broken, and the flushing mechanism leaked water onto the floor. When I came out again, the radio was playing "Oh Schnucki, oh Schnucki, let's travel to Kentucky ..." Hertha swayed in rhythm with the tune. The guy at the bar used his snot rag again. Then he grabbed his glass with both hands and knocked back the schnapps in one go. He slammed the glass back onto the counter.

"Hertha! One more."

"Now, now, Karl. You've had enough."

Karl pulled a wrinkled fifty-mark bill out of his pocket.

"You think I can't pay? Is that what you think?"

"Put your money back."

Hertha arranged the rinsed glasses on the shelf. Karl lit a cigarette. After a while he glanced at me.

"Gladbach, eh?"

I nodded. He scrutinized me from head to toe. Then he turned away, growling, "Well, this is Frankfurt."

The radio was playing "When Heidi and her Hans, tah-rah, tah-rah ..." I picked the newspaper off the rack.

"FRANKFURT TRIAL BEGINS WITH EXTENSIVE SECURITY MEASURES. The trial of four members of the Ecological Front begins behind closed doors." It was a quarter to nine. I paid and left Hertha's Corner.

Outside, the wind was driving the rain diagonally across the street. Fall. I pulled the brim of my hat down, dug my hands into my coat pockets, and stayed close to the wall. At the intersection, the furious rain whipped my face, and water began to slosh in my shoes. Everything looked gray. Only a few neon signs interrupted the dreariness of the concrete wasteland. Empty cans, milk cartons, cigarette butts, garbage floated down the gutters and got stuck in the drains. There were streaks of dog shit on the sidewalk. People with umbrellas charged past me. Women stood chatting in the doorways, waiting for the rain to let up. I could feel my coat getting drenched. A taxicab splashed puddles onto my pants. I kept going, slipping on cartons and vegetable refuse, until I reached the courthouse steps. The door fell shut behind me. Like a leaking bucket, I left a wet track on the stone floor.

"Halt!"

Two cops barred my way. I pulled out my private investigator's license.

"I have an appointment with Dr. Anastas."

"We don't know him."

"He's the defendants' attorney."

"Unh-hunh."

A squad was pacing up and down the hall, submachine guns at the ready. The cop looked up from my license.

"Your I.D."

I showed it to him. His companion scratched his chin, raised his walkie-talkie, and recited my I.D. number into it. After he received the all clear, I had to spread my legs.

They didn't find anything. "Upstairs, second door on the left," they told me. A bunch of journalists were lounging in the waiting room, which smelled of cold tobacco smoke and wet clothes. They were all chattering away with supreme self-importance. A pretty thing with long dark hair sat down next to me.

"Cold, isn't it?"

She sniffled.

"Sure is."

She snuggled down into her fur coat.

"What paper you with?"

"My Wife and Your Car."

"I see." Pause. "Don't know that one."

I lit a cigarette.

"May I have one?"

I lit it for her. We smoked for a while. What did that attorney want from me? Why had he asked me to be here so early? She was studying my profile. I leaned back and closed my eyes.

"You're not a journalist."

"Right you are."

"I can tell."

"I see. How?"

"Well, you have no camera, you don't talk, you don't know anybody, and now you're taking a nap."

She smelled nice. Something heavy, from France.

"Nonsense. I'm a Turk. That's how you can tell."

She ground out the cigarette under her heel.

"Maybe." Pause. "So—why are you here?"

"I'm a private investigator. Don't ask me why, I just am. And I'm waiting for someone."

Now there was a commotion by the door. Cameras were focused, note pads raised.

"A private investigator—and a Turk? I'm supposed to believe that?"

"Take it or leave it."

The noise level rose. The pack was straining at the leash. My avenging angel moved closer.

"Have you been living in Germany for a long time?"

"My father was one of the first Turkish garbage collectors of this republic. He brought me here when I was a year old. Soon after that, he was run over by a car. I was adopted by a German family."

"And your mother?"

"She died when I was born."

She mimed compassion.

"Oh, how terrible."

I pointed at the door.

At that moment, the double doors to the courtroom swung open and the reporters charged. She took her leave and dived into the melee. There was a lot of noise in the hallway. I stayed put and contemplated my soaked shoes. Then I too entered the courtroom. The attorney was answering questions from a group of newspaper people. Cameras flashed incessantly, camcorders jockeyed for position. Off in a corner, a guy was broadcasting live, manically yelling into his mike. Policemen were posted by doors and windows. I sat down on a bench. My clothes were wet and stuck to my skin. The place was drafty, and I was cold. I lit a cigarette and watched the court clerk, who was waving his arms at me from a distance, presumably to indicate that smoking was prohibited. Ten o'clock. Five minutes later, the attorney walked over and sat down next to me.

"Please forgive me, Mr. Kayankaya. You know, in a trial of this importance ... One has to humor the press. I'm sure you understand."

Dr. Anastas was small and sturdy. Everything about him was brown: the curls around his balding pate, the frame of the eyeglasses resting on the bridge of his snub nose, his suit, his fingernails. His tie drooped like a wet towel.

"Why did you ask me to come here at nine o'clock?"

He frowned.

"I did? I thought we agreed on ten. I'm sorry."

He stared pensively into the courtroom, which was emptying out. Even the cops were picking up their things and leaving.

"You wanted to see me."

He gave a start.

"Forgive me, I have to keep track of so many things. Maybe ..."

"Why don't we go and have a cup of coffee?"

He deliberated, then raised a hand to his forehead.

"Excellent idea. Let's. I agreed to meet someone in a restaurant just around the corner. What's it called? Something with an O in it. I'm sure we can find it. After all, you're a detective."

He laughed and patted my shoulder, bounded to his feet, and trotted off. I pulled my damp coat around my shoulders and followed.

.2.

"That's it, over there! Chez Jules. No O in that. Doesn't matter. We found it."

He parked, and we went inside. It was one of those nouveau joints where you're afraid the table might collapse if you set down a decent glass of beer on it. You sit on tiny chairs, munch on tidbits, drink out of little glasses. Everything has dainty legs—the furniture, the ladies, the candlesticks. You say "pardon" when you sit down at a table and "ciao" when you get up again. The habitués call out things like, "Jules, are the crabs fresh today?"

The place was packed with a lunchtime crowd. Anastas hurried through it, his neck stretched like a chicken's, looking for his date. Sipping white wine and nibbling on slices of roasted garlic, the stylish ladies and gentlemen cast pitying glances at the little lawyer. I could hear them whispering to each other. Anastas waved to me and shouted, "Over here, Mr. Kayankaya!" It wouldn't have surprised me to see the patrons fall off their chairs. As I joined Anastas, I recognized my pretty inquisitor from the courthouse. She looked at me and laughed.

"Oh, it's the private eye. Now I understand."

"You do?"

Anastas looked astounded.

"You've met before?"

"Just briefly. Not long enough to exchange names."

"Carla Reedermann of the *Rundblick.* Kemal Kayankaya."

We nodded and slid onto chairs. Carla Reedermann smiled.

"What a coincidence."

"Yes. Indeed."

I lit a cigarette and hid behind the menu. Anastas slid his eyeglasses to the tip of his nose and perused the offerings three times over. A waiter, bouncy in white tennis shoes, ambled over, stopped casually by our table, and asked for our orders. Anastas ordered two cheese baguettes and two tomato salads. Then he removed his glasses, folded his hands, and smiled at me.

"So here we are, Mr. Kayankaya."

"Here we are."

Contentedly he stroked his balding pate. I stared at his round head and pondered why I had been up and about since eight o'clock. The waiter returned with our plates. With a broad grin, Anastas wished us bon appétit and attacked his first baguette.

I stirred milk and sugar into my coffee, poured my shot of Scotch into it, and took a long sip. My egg on toast was lukewarm and tasted like a fried egg wrapped in brown paper, but the little lawyer was really enjoying his food. His tongue was angling for the threads of cheese that had strayed onto his face, his teeth mashing the greasy white bread. He washed it all down with black coffee. A thick slice of tomato slid off his fork—he sucked it right off his tie. When he asked me if my toast was all right, I pushed it aside and lit a cigarette. Carla Reedermann was working on her order of mussels. I wondered about her connection to this gluttonous little fellow. Her brown eyes kept glancing provocatively at me. I ordered another coffee and Scotch. The two of them chewed their food in silence. I constructed houses out of beer coasters. Five minutes later, the waiter brought my coffee. Anastas reached for the menu to place another order. I slammed the beer coasters onto the table. "Now, wait a minute! I didn't get up at that ungodly hour just to watch you have lunch."

The waiter made himself scarce. Anastas put the menu down, wiped his lips, and put his glasses back on.

"I'm sorry."

"And I don't want any reporters."

I pointed at the newspaper woman. After a moment's silence, she pushed the plate of mussels aside, put a twenty-mark note on the table, and went to get her coat.

Anastas followed her with his eyes.

"Mr. Kayankaya, Miss Reedermann is on my side. I'm sure she won't write anything that ..."

"You can do as you please. I prefer working alone."

She returned, picked up her purse, and left. She was furious.

"So. What's the story?"

Anastas adjusted his glasses and murmured, "You must have read about the Ecological Front's act of sabotage?"

"Not a whole lot."

"As you know, I am defending the four people involved. I have been working on the case for months. I still haven't found a concept that would enable me to mount a successful defense. My clients pretty much refuse to make statements. They treat me kindly, but they won't tell me more than they're willing to tell the prosecutor. They openly admit that they did blow up the waste pipe of the Böllig chemical plant in Doddelbach. The firm is about forty years old, a medium-sized family enterprise. Twenty years ago, Friedrich Böllig inherited it from his father, who died relatively young. Six months ago, at the time of the explosion, Friedrich Böllig was killed. His body was found with four bullets in his chest and head, on the grounds of the plant, not far from the detonated waste pipe. My clients deny that they even set eyes on him, much less shot him. I believe them. First of all, they had no motive, and second, these four are as far removed from killer commandos as a delegation of allotment holders would be."

"You don't know those allotment holders ..."

"They only wanted to destroy one of Böllig's waste pipes. Material damage, nothing else."

"What kind of waste did the pipes dispose of?"

"Chemical waste products, just like everywhere else.

But some kids in the region developed strange skin problems, and the matter had been taken up with the Böllig firm. These children had been bathing in the lake into which those waste products were discharged. There were all kinds of initiatives, but none of them led to any change. My clients wanted to do something to get the debate going again."

"And they were successful."

"Yes ... But it seems like they themselves don't really know what to think about the whole thing." He chewed pensively on a tomato slice. "It must be a strange feeling. You go and blow up a concrete pipe, and the next day's papers tell you that someone has been shot and killed."

"Did they find the gun?"

"No."

"Let me see if I got this straight. In the middle of the night, four people detonate a waste pipe belonging to the Böllig plant, and a few steps away, and at the same time, the head of that enterprise is shot and killed. And just because your clients look so pitiful when you visit them in their cells, you can't see a connection ... But how to convince the court of that? Good luck, is all I can say. What do you need me for?"

"The fifth man is missing. According to witnesses, *five* people participated in the action."

"Witnesses?"

"A fellow was camping by the lakeshore, not far from the plant. With his girlfriend. The explosion woke him up, and as he rushed out of his tent, he saw *five* people running away."

"What do you clients have to say about that?"

"Nothing. They don't want to betray their comrade. But I believe that he is the key to this case, and that is why I want to hire you. Today I asked for a postponement of the trial date, to give you time to find the man. One week, exactly."

I ground my cigarette into the ashtray.

"So you need a private investigator. Why me? I'm a Turk."

His stubby fingers scratched the back of his other hand. "I read about your last case. I think you're pretty incorruptible."

"Depends on the size of the bribe ..."

"What I mean is that you're not easily swayed by public opinion. If you take this on, you have to be incorruptible in that sense."

Pause. It took him at least three minutes to come out with his next question.

"How did you end up in this profession? Being a Turk, I mean ..."

"I'm a citizen of the Federal Republic."

"Oh, I see."

He nodded, and as he leaned forward, there was a glint of solidarity in his eyes.

"Not so easy to acquire, that damn citizenship, is it?"

"No problem. I mow my lawn, I laugh a lot during the carnival season, and I manage to drink beer and play skat at the same time. Somewhere past Munich lies Africa, that's where the Negroes live. I hate interruptions during sportscasts. My living-room set has been paid for. And I'm really a dancing Silesian at heart."

For a moment he seemed on the verge of the inevitable "You must be kidding," but he restrained himself and only gave an affected laugh.

"Seriously, Mr. Kayankaya—how long have you been living in Germany?"

"My mother died after she gave birth to me. My father took me to Germany. He didn't last very long, and I was adopted by a German family. I've lived in this country for as long as I can remember."

He nodded.

"Forgive me. That's quite a story."

I lit a cigarette.

"It is?"

I took a drag.

"You should have heard the one I told my last client."

I blew smoke rings.

"How did they find your defendants?"

"*That* is one of many dubious aspects in the case."

"Meaning what?"

"Meaning that the police simply stormed their apartment three days after the explosion. There had been no search to speak of."

"Maybe someone squealed."

"Yes ..."

"Could have been that fifth man."

"Maybe ..."

"The police didn't say how they managed to find the suspects so quickly?"

"The man in charge, Detective Superintendent Kessler, was quite reticent about it. He merely said that the suspects had been arrested at the end of a quickly organized investigation."

"Not a word about the fifth man?"

"Not a word."

"Are they looking for him now?"

"I assume they are."

"On what grounds?"

"Well, he's just as suspect as my clients are."

"What if he made a little deal with the cops? His freedom for the address of your clients?"

"I don't think so. Not in a case that has attracted so much political attention. The police can't afford it."

"All right. So the cops are after him—but you think you need a P.I. to chase him too. Who do you think I am? If the guy has half a brain, he's made tracks, and not just from Sachsenhausen to the North End or the other way round, but much farther. If you like, I'll take your money and drive around. But it's a bit out of my league."

"In my opinion, a discreet loner may be more effective. Naturally I'll take care of your expenses ..."

He hesitated.

"If I didn't think you were a good detective—I would have got up and left long ago."

"I've been sitting around in these wet rags for three hours. I can't stand it when people smack their lips while eating. And I would have preferred to meet your friend alone, on a night with a full moon."

"You were none too kind to Miss Reedermann."

"There was no full moon, either."

"Furthermore, in this case ... I don't know your political views, but ..."

"I'm just supposed to find this guy, right?"

"Yes, of course, but political views do come into play. People want to see my clients convicted. So-called Green terrorists are grist to the mill for the Right. They're the best thing that could have happened, from the Rightists' point of view. Considering the business with the Rhein Main Farben plant, and ..."

"All right. To set your mind at rest, I really believe that

hand-knitted socks, free-range chickens, and argumentative women are terrific. I don't look good in seal fur. But don't ask me for the next paper recycling date."

"Well, then." He sighed. "So you accept?"

"Two hundred marks a day plus expenses."

"No reduced rates for a good cause?"

"It's included. *I* am the good cause."

He nodded, looking a little sour. "How do you intend to start?"

"First I'll have a word with your clients. Then I'll drive to Doppenburg."

"My clients? But that's out of the question. They refuse to talk to anyone but me."

"In that case, I need official reports, background information, and so on." I considered this for a moment.

"The Böllig plant doesn't employ a night watchman?"

"He was knocked out."

"And?"

"He saw the person. At a lineup, he didn't recognize a single one of my clients."

"The fifth man?"

I stood up and pocketed my pack of cigarettes. "When can I see you in your office?"

"Tonight."

"Around eight, then. Where is Doppenburg?"

"On the Frankfurt-Heidelberg freeway, past Darmstadt. It has its own exit."

"I'll see you tonight. See if you can make that lakeside camper be there too."

I left. The sky had lightened and the rain had slackened to a drizzle. A couple of small clouds stuck to the tall downtown buildings like dirty cottonballs. I turned up my coat collar and hurried to the nearest subway station.

·3·

I pushed the front door and turned on the light in the entrance hall. Almost instantly the greengrocer popped out of his ground-floor apartment. In his corduroy slippers, turned-up jeans, and green nylon pullover, he barred my way, his shiny blond hair combed severely to the right. He was waving an empty cigarette pack excitedly.

"What is this? Tell me, what is this?"

His head bounced forward and back, as if pummeled from behind by an invisible fist.

One more time. "What is this?"

I unlocked my mailbox.

"I have no idea."

"It is an empty cigarette pack, and I found it this morning, on the landing! Because *I sweep* my landing! Do you hear me? I sweep my landing! Here in Germany, we sweep our landings! We're not in the Balkans here, and you better get used to it, or else go back there! You terrorize the whole building with your garbage ... the whole building!"

He jabbed the pack with his index finger as if to punch holes in it. "All the other tenants have confirmed that this is the brand you smoke. Well, what do you have to say to that? Well?"

He raised his eyebrows and went on ranting.

"Ha! That strikes you dumb, doesn't it! But let me tell you something—if ever again I find one of these on the landing, I'll get the owner and show him the mess. Your mess! Then you'll have to deal with *him*. Do you understand?"

I felt like pasting him.

"Come on, say something! You're always such a smartass, how come you don't know what to say?"

I took the mail out of my box, locked it again, and advanced. We were still two meters apart when he began to stammer.

"If you do anything to me ... if you dare ... I'll, I'll call the police ... and they, they'll arrest you, and there'll be some peace in this building, at long last ... They'll put you in jail, and we'll be rid of you!"

He fluttered his hands in front of me like a man shooing off pigeons.

"Now, now ... I'm warning you ... if you touch me, I'll ... I'll call for help ..."

He was out of breath. I pushed past him and climbed the stairs to my apartment. Once inside, I pulled off my damp clothes and took a hot shower. I had an unpleasant prickling sensation in my feet. Drying myself off, I thought about Carla Reedermann. Then I put on a pair of wool pants and two pullovers and a pair of hiking boots. The kitchen smelled of burnt onions. I poured myself a tumbler of Chivas and went to the phone. I dialed the number of my garage and listened to the phone ring for a while.

"Riebl Auto Repair."

"Kayankaya. Is my car ready?"

"I'm just working on it."

"It's been three weeks since you told me you'd have it ready for me in a week."

"Not to worry, I'll have it fixed the day after tomorrow at the latest."

"I'm not worried. I need a car today, and if you can't do it, I'll take your limo."

He giggled. Riebl was one of those people who seem

to be drunk all the time while never touching a drop of the stuff. He was just a little goofy.

"That's no joke. I'll be there in half an hour."

He kept on giggling and mumbled something. I hung up.

"Be right there."

Riebl was lying under the hood of my green Opel Kadett. The place smelled of gasoline and lubricant. A radio in a corner was screeching tunes of the German homeland. Then he surfaced.

"Oh, it's you, Mr...."

"Kayankaya."

"Right."

"What's with my car?"

He scratched his neck and stared absently at the floor, as if he had just heard an immoral proposition.

"We-ell ..."

"Well, what?"

"You know, it's so easy to make a wrong estimate. At first it just seems to be the sparks, but then it turns out the whole engine is screwy. You know what I mean?"

"Give me the keys to your car. I'll be back tonight, at half past seven."

He shook his pinched head.

"Tch, tch, tch, I don't know ..."

"Come on."

Hesitantly he produced a bunch of keys out of a pocket of his overalls.

"But really ... I don't ..."

"See you tonight."

I left him standing next to my Kadett. Twenty kilometers past Darmstadt, I took the Doppenburg exit.

.4.

I first heard it from a guy with red hair in the Zum Grossen Schiff tavern in Sachsenhausen: He insisted on calling the place Dopeyburg, not Doppenburg. However, since he also pronounced "cider" "soyder," I didn't pay much attention, but later I noticed that other people of more cultivated speech habits also referred to the place by that pejorative name. Well, I thought, just another instance of that rather less than brilliant sense of humor that turns a professor into a perfesser. Only now, years later and on site in Doppenburg, did I realize how appropriate it was.

Doppenburg was a small town centered around an ugly pedestrian mall. Supermarkets were interspersed with third-rate fashion shops staffed by saleswomen who resembled the sausages in the butcher's window. Flower planters, round light fixtures, and empty benches adorned the street. Retired people pulled their shopping bags on carts across the pavement, probably attracted by some advertised sale in spite of the wet and the cold. In sheltered corners, housewives discussed the problems of noodle casseroles, children, and varicose veins. At one end of this parody of an urban environment stood the inevitable Italian ice-cream café frequented by Coke-guzzling teenagers perched on their motorbikes, cradling helmets under one arm and cracking bad jokes about their girls.

I parked the car on the main street and strolled uphill into the old part of town, with its rows of half-timbered houses that looked as if children had modeled them out of clay, then baked and neatly painted them. Immaculate streets. Not even the smallest pile of dog shit to offend German cleanliness. Except for a couple of shiny pink tea and health shops, the streets were dead. A young man stood at a deserted intersection waiting for the traffic light to turn green. When he saw me cross against the red, his lips tightened disapprovingly. I think he would have liked to follow me in order to punch me in the face, for the sake of law and Fatherland, but the light didn't change.

At a refreshment kiosk I asked for directions to the Böllig plant. Two guys stood there in the rain, drinking their dinner.

They grinned.

"Böllisch? With his broken pipe?"

He slapped his companion's shoulder.

"Our pipes are broken too. Right, Ennst? What does the Mrs. say to that? Hey, Ennst! Broken pipe!"

"How do I get there?"

"Böllisch ... Hey, Ennst! How does he get there? Ennst!"

Ernst squinted at me slyly and said, almost choking with mirth, "And how do I get to the opera?"

"Practice. A lot of practice," I said, and walked away.

"Har, har. That was a good one. The old ones are the best ones."

The baker's wife gave me directions. I walked back to the car and followed the flow of traffic down the main street toward Weinheim. After a kilometer or so, tall brick walls appeared by the side of the road, their tops covered with barbed wire: Ruhenbrunn Private Clinic. Just past those walls was the paved entry road to the Böllig plant.

The factory stood on a hillside, with the notorious lake to its right. The dirty yellow water lapped gently against the bright gravel on the shore.

I stumbled across the little wet rocks to the demolished waste pipe. Such concrete pipes did not require major amounts of explosives for their destruction. The action must have been about as exciting as a flat tire in a no-parking zone. I contemplated the shoreline. Where the gravel ended, small clumps of reeds separated the moldering soil from the water. It seemed an unlikely site to choose for a camping trip. I turned around. The factory was a pile of corrugated iron. Out of it, at seemingly random intervals, rose three mighty smokestacks. On top of one of them, a thin flame flickered. On the side of a warehouse, a row of faded red letters proclaimed that this was BÖLLIG DRUGS—FOR LIFE, FOR THE FUTURE, FOR OUR CHILDREN. Chemical enterprises have a weakness for hyperbolic publicity.

"Hey, you! What are you doing there? This is factory property!"

A skinny fellow wearing a sea captain's cap came running across the gravel and stopped in front of me, breathing hard.

"Just looking around. The site of that sabotage."

"You can't just walk in like that. Do you have a permit?"

"I'm investigating the matter for the public prosecutor's office."

He scratched his chin.

"You are?"

"I am."

"But you don't look the type."

"So?"

"The public prosecutor's office, that's an important office, to do with the law and all ... But really, you look ... I'm sorry. If you're really working for them ..."

He fussed with the sleeves of his uniform jacket.

"Are you the night watchman?"

"Yes, that's my job."

"You were knocked out, a while ago?"

"Yes, I was."

His knees were twitching, and he kept looking back at the factory buildings, as if he were afraid he could be seen from there.

"You saw the man?"

He was trying hard not to avoid my eyes.

"I already told the police all about it."

"So you saw the man?"

"Yes, I did."

Once again his eyes turned toward the factory.

"What did he look like?"

"He didn't look like anything. He had something over his head, a stocking or a cap, I couldn't tell. It was dark."

"Let's take it from the top. You were on your rounds, and he just came out of nowhere and hit you over the head?"

"No ... you see, I was sitting in my cabin, over there ..."

He pointed behind his back. As he went on talking, he looked more and more troubled.

"... I was reading, whatever ... and suddenly the door slams open, and before I had time to turn around, I was hit over the head, and it was lights out for me. When I came to my senses, the police had arrived. And that was all there was to it."

The wind had risen to blow the drizzling rain across the field. I lit a cigarette and let him squirm a little.

"It was dark, and you didn't have time to turn around? That's strange. This morning, someone told me there had been a lineup of suspects ... Was he just putting me on?"

"No, there was a lineup, all right. But ... Why don't you ask the police? They have all the information."

"And he was wearing a stocking over his head. Maybe you should have sent your wife to that lineup."

"But see, the superintendent had arranged that lineup just as, like, a shot in the dark."

He raised his hat and wiped his forehead.

"When you came to, the police were there? Immediately? You opened your eyes and saw green uniforms?"

"What? No. Mrs. Böllig arrived first. She woke me up, so to speak. They live right there, you see."

"When Mrs. Böllig woke you up—had she already found her husband?"

"I don't know ... I think ..."

"Don't you think a woman would mention it if she had just found her husband riddled with bullets?"

"Everything happened so fast, and ... but you're right, I remember now. Yes, she was falling apart, she was hardly able to utter a sensible word ..."

He smiled at me cautiously. Following classic cop procedure, I took out my cigarette pack and offered him one. He lit up and we smoked. As soon as he looked a little more relaxed, I resumed my questioning. "He must have hit you hard."

"Yes, with a club. I can still feel it."

"I see. May I take a look?"

His eyes opened wide.

"Come again?"

"I'd like to see where he clubbed you. Come on."

He took off his cap in slow motion.

"But ... after six months? Of course it's healed over by now."

"When you get hit like that, you keep the scars for life," I said, and after I had checked his head and found no marks, "All right."

I said no more as we strode across the wet gravel to the factory, passing barrels, pipes, and trucks, walking through a shed filled with huge stacks of numbered crates, turning a corner next to a forklift, and finally reemerging back into the rain through a large doorway. The Villa Böllig stood a hundred meters farther away on a hillside. It was a luxurious white bungalow with a roof garden and a tennis court to one side. Bushy little Christmas trees dotted the English lawn, which had a pile of scrap metal as its centerpiece. A silver Mercedes convertible was parked in front of the garage, next to a black compact.

I took my leave of the night watchman, assuring him that I would drop by again soon. I crossed the parking lot and reached the wrought-iron gate guarding the paved driveway that snaked across the lawn. A bell and an intercom were embedded in a marble gatepost. I pushed the brass button and waited for the German shepherd, but the only growl I heard emanated from the intercom speaker. "Who is it?"

"Kayankaya. From the public prosecutor's office in Frankfurt."

"The prosecutor's office?"

This was followed by a moment's silence. Someone shouted. Then the voice returned.

"Come on in."

The buzzer sounded, and I pushed the gate. The pile of scrap metal turned out to be a work of art; I thought I could discern some intertwined fish shapes, but couldn't be sure. The layout, including the house, had the atmosphere of an abandoned first-class service area along the freeway. When I arrived at the front door, I used the antique door knocker and was immediately and unexpectedly admitted by an attractive blonde in her forties.

"How do you do? I'm Barbara Böllig. What can I do for you?"

Her voluptuous body was sheathed in a plain black wool dress that clung tightly around her hips. Her hair was tied back with a glittery red ribbon. Her green eyes scrutinized me.

"Kayankaya, from the public prosecutor's office in Frankfurt. I have to ask you a couple of questions." It didn't look as if she would grace me with the enchanting smile of which her mouth looked quite capable. She crossed her solarium-tanned arms over her chest and cocked her head.

"I don't know that I have anything left to tell you."

"Do you always let callers stay out in the rain?"

"When they call at an inconvenient time."

She seemed disinclined to let me into the house. I looked at it. I looked at the garden.

"So, all of this is now yours?"

"So what?"

I pointed at the cars.

"Those too?"

"The Mini belongs to a friend."

"Who is standing by your side during these difficult months?"

"If you wish."

"So you don't feel that you're lacking in support?"

"I beg your pardon?"

"People tend to be particularly solicitous of pretty widows who own factories. It's the dream of all divisional managers, isn't it? The boss croaks, and his lady looks for a successor. In every which way."

Bang, the door fell shut. I hammered on it long enough for it to fly open again. A colossal guy emerged. Two meters tall and about as wide, weighing in at about two hundred pounds, he was wearing basketball shoes and a gray sweatsuit. His head was shaved.

"What's the problem?"

As he spoke, his arms swung gently back and forth. One wrist was adorned by one of those gold chains with an engraved name tag. How did he manage to get into that Mini?

"I came here to speak to Mrs. Böllig."

He protruded his lower lip and raised his eyebrows.

"She's feeling a little indisposed today. Why don't you come back some other time?"

"She looked pretty healthy just a minute ago."

Before he could say anything to that, the widow called out from inside the house, "Let him come in, Henry."

Henry turned his head, shrugged, and let me in. I waded across the carpet, past a telephone table and a coat rack, and into the large living room. Its rear wall was glass and opened onto a view of a garden area that looked just like the one in front of the house—the only difference being that it ended, after about fifty meters, in the brick wall of the private clinic. The decor bespoke too much money and too little taste: furniture from every century, pale blue wallpaper, three layers of Iranian carpets, Indian lamp shades, and so on. The widow was reclining on a leather settee, sipping a yellow drink. Henry pushed me into an armchair, pulled up a chair, and seated himself behind me. I began to wonder whether this towering fellow was a lover or a bodyguard. Probably both. Ladies seem to enjoy bodybuilders in sweatsuits with little gold chains around their wrists. The widow set her glass down.

"What to you want to know? I thought all the questions had been answered by now."

"The trial began today. Did you know that?"

"I read the papers."

"All right. Now, there still are a few gaps in the prosecution's case, and that is why I need you to tell me, once again, *exactly* what happened that night. There just may be something we've overlooked."

She sucked her finger pensively.

"Are you always that persistent?"

"Depends on the weather. Please—tell me one more time what happened before your husband ran over there, to the factory."

She sat up straight. The wool dress showed off her tanned knees. My attention wandered for a few seconds.

"I'm not sure I can remember everything. It's been six months ..." Then, after a pause:

"We were watching television, Friedrich and I. I was falling asleep. Then suddenly he jumps up and runs to the door. And while he's pulling on his coat he shouts to me that he's heard an explosion or something, and then—"

"You hadn't heard anything?"

"No, I was half asleep. So Friedrich ran off, and I stayed here in the living room. When he didn't return—"

"For how long?"

"Fifteen minutes or so ... I went out and started calling for him. And then, after a while, I found him."

She sounded bored; she wasn't even pretending grief.

"Where?"

"Near that pipe. Maybe ten meters from it."

"What did you do then?"

"I ran over to Scheigel, the night watchman, and found

him lying on the floor, unconscious. When he came to, we called the police."

"You didn't happen to notice his head injury?"

She gave me a suspicious look.

"Listen, I had just found my husband murdered. I didn't feel like playing nurse."

I rubbed my chin and thought about the drink I had not been offered.

"Which means nobody paid any attention to that."

"What do you mean?"

"I just had a word with Scheigel. No one examined his head after the attack."

She raised her eyebrows.

"Careless of him. Head injuries can be dangerous."

"That's what I've been thinking."

I could feel Henry breathing down my neck. Mrs. Böllig ran the tip of her index finger around the edge of her glass. The ice cubes clinked quietly.

"How long were you married to Friedrich Böllig?"

"Sixteen years. We were married on the eighteenth of January, nineteen sixty-nine."

"Your father-in-law was deceased at that time?"

"He was."

"How old was your husband when he became the head of the firm?"

"Twenty-eight."

"And when you got married?"

"Thirty-one."

"And how old were you?"

She sat up straight.

"Is that any of your business?"

"Let that be my worry. How old were you?"

"Nineteen."

"How did you meet your husband?"

"I was his secretary."

"I see."

Henry was breathing more loudly.

"Were you fond of him?"

She slammed her glass down on the cocktail table. A vein started throbbing at her temple.

"That's enough! Get out."

"Do you have children?"

A leaden weight descended onto my shoulder.

"Come on, friend, I'll walk you to the door."

I turned. "Hands off." To her: "*Do* you have any?"

"I have a son."

"How old is he? What does he do?"

"He is seventeen. He was born handicapped, and he lives in an institution. Will that do?"

She jumped up and towered above me like one of the Furies. It was clear that the handicapped child was a blemish in this solarium-tanned facade of fast cars, expensive parties, and good-looking tennis coaches. But then, probably any child would have been a blemish.

"Did your husband do business with other firms?"

That stopped her. This was not the question that would have led to my instant eviction.

"Sometimes."

"Were there particularly close relations with some of them?"

She charged across the room.

"God almighty, of course there were! My husband did business with a lot of people. Check the books. Go see Meyer—he's the business manager."

I poked the last cigarette out of my pack.

"Was your husband the sole proprietor of Böllig Chemicals?"

"I held thirty percent."

"Now you've got a hundred."

I smoked, and Friedrich's widow leaned against the glass wall and contemplated the wet trees in her yard. She still looked really good. So good that I had to force myself out of the chair. Henry rose too, a small cigar dangling from the corner of his mouth.

"Mr. Meyer's office is over there?"

"Yes."

"All right. That's it, for the time being."

We parted. It was still drizzling outside. I estimated the distance from the driveway to the waste pipe. It was considerable, and I asked myself why five people who had just committed an act of sabotage against an industrial enterprise would stick around and wait for the owner to appear on the scene.

"Mr. Meyer? Room number twenty-eight."

I walked up the stairs and knocked on the door. Someone sneezed, then said, "Come in." I opened the door and found myself in a reception area. The secretary behind the desk held a handkerchief to her nose and looked at me as if I were some long-extinct reptile. She was in her twenties and had a blond perm, freckles, and pink heart-shaped earrings. Every German country boy's dream. A collection of postcards had been taped to the wall behind her.

"This is Mr. Meyer's office?"

"Do you have an appointment?"

"Mrs. Böllig sent me."

"I see ... Let me check."

With one hand, she depressed a key on her intercom;

with the other, she went on working on her nose, all the while eyeing me suspiciously. Finally someone came on the line.

"Mr. Meyer, I have a gentleman here who wants to see you. He says Mrs. Böllig sent him ... I don't know ... He's not from here ... No, I mean he's not from here at all, if you know what I mean. Very well, Mr. Meyer." She looked up.

"Have a seat, please. Mr. Meyer is still on the phone."

I sat down on the visitors' banquette. It was getting dark outside, and the village princess switched the light on. While I rummaged in my pockets for cigarettes, in vain, she cast a surreptitious glance at me, moved her own pack of HBs into a drawer, and went back to her papers. Finally the door opened and Mr. Meyer peered out.

"Yes?"

I got up.

"Kayankaya, from the public prosecutor's office. I'm investigating the Böllig case, and I need to take a look at your business records. For various reasons. Mrs. Böllig suggested that I talk to you."

When she heard me mentioning the prosecutor's office, the princess looked flabbergasted. Meyer, embarrassed, compressed his lips.

"The prosecutor's office? I see. I thought we were done with all that. The murderers have been apprehended, haven't they? But all right, you have to do what you have to do. I was getting ready to go home, but ..."

He was a head shorter than I, skinny and wiry. In his blue corduroy suit and elevator shoes, he looked as if he had been to the dry cleaners. When he spoke, his ears wagged. An electronic timer dangled from his wrist, and he kept moving it tenderly up and down his arm.

"I'm sorry, Mr. Meyer, I'm just doing my job."

He liked that.

"As we all are. Come on in, Mr.—what was the name again?"

"Kayankaya."

"Very good. Come in."

Before he closed the door, he cast another glance at the princess.

"Petra? Could you be so kind and stay on for a while? We have a few more things to discuss." He twinkled paternally at her bosom, closed the door, and strutted over to his desk.

"What can I do for you, Mr. Kayankaya?"

"I need all the records on business connections with other enterprises, starting from nineteen sixty-six. I also need to see the complete and up-to-date personnel and payroll records. And the financial records and balance sheets, also dating back to sixty-six."

He had stopped gnawing on his lower lip. He put a piece of peppermint candy in his mouth.

"That's quite a task you've taken on there."

"The sooner I start, the sooner I'll be done."

He nodded.

"That's what I always tell my people. Procrastination destroys morale and is bad for the firm. You know what I mean?"

I didn't.

"Just a moment. I'll have the files brought here."

Five minutes later, a man arrived with a mountainous stack of ring binders. Without any idea of what I was looking for, I started turning pages. Meyer seemed impatient; his plans for a little overtime with Petra were obviously evaporating. Finally I decided to look at the payroll records. There is something sensuous about money, even if it belongs to other people.

"Why is Dr. Kliensmann making three times as much as anyone else?"

"Dr. Kliensmann is not involved in development or research or production. He acts as a psychological consultant to the firm and its staff. It was the late Mr. Böllig's idea to employ him in that capacity, in accordance with the American model."

"How does that work? Does the doctor have a room with a couch here at the factory, so that anyone who wants to, or has to, may go there and get things off their chest?"

Meyer smiled.

"No, no. Dr. Kliensmann is the director of Ruhenbrunn—you may have noticed the clinic on your way here? In urgent cases he'll come over, but mostly his task consists in advising the administration on their treatment of employees. As, for instance, how to motivate the will to work, or how to create an atmosphere in which people identify with the firm and give it their best. Dr. Kliensmann is also consulted on matters such as our new cafeteria space. You know, the Japanese have really discovered amazing things about all that."

"And the doctor's advice is as expensive as that?"

"It's a matter of rewarding quality, not quantity."

I looked at a few more pages. Then I decided that I had seen enough.

"I'm done with these, Mr. Meyer. But could I see your records on the unfortunate events of last summer? I need the addresses of the children involved, the amounts sued for, the court decisions in each case, and so on."

"Just a moment."

Meyer left the office. Through the half-open door, I

heard him suggest that the princess go on to his place. I took another look at the files. When he returned with a red folder and put it on the table, I held up the personnel list.

"A Mr. Windelen and a Dr. Hahn were dismissed last month. Why?"

"A most unpleasant affair. Windelen and Hahn repeatedly, and without consulting with management, meddled in the debate about that poison business. Even within the firm, they demanded the creation of some kind of investigative and control committee for waste-water matters. They so poisoned the working atmosphere of our firm that it became unbearable."

I examined the red folder. The damages sued for in the case of each child amounted to fifty thousand marks. Medical reports stated that they had suffered permanent skin damage. The trial date was set for next February.

"Why don't you just pay up? That would remove you from the public eye."

He gave me a searching look.

"Since Mr. Böllig was murdered, we stand a pretty good chance of winning the case. Public opinion has turned around."

"Oh, I see."

"Don't get me wrong, now. We never felt responsible for the accident in the first place. There are fences, there are signs warning of possible danger. Besides, the lake is on factory grounds. One might say that those children entered it illegally."

"If you lost the case, you'd have to pay four hundred and fifty thousand marks. Is that a large sum for Böllig Chemicals to come up with?"

"I think we'd survive. But we could, of course, find better uses for the money. We are a family concern, and that's rare these days. We operate on a very narrow margin."

"Mrs. Böllig now owns the company, one hundred percent."

"One hundred percent, that is, of the Böllig family's shares. Those constitute sixty percent of the total. The remainder is held by various shareholders."

"Are you a shareholder?"

He stroked his chin, then leaned closer.

"Confidentially speaking—it wouldn't be a smart investment. Too risky. A single miscalculation could endanger the survival of the firm. Shares in such enterprises are for people who like to take a gamble. You would have to bet on the chance that, for instance, one of our chemists comes up with something really big."

"Such as?"

"Whatever—let's say, an internationally recognized hair restorative."

"What about those four hundred and fifty thou? Could they be a major mishap?"

"They could set a decline in motion. Not to mention the loss of goodwill with the public, if we lost the case."

"So one might say—from a purely economic point of view—that Mr. Böllig's sensational assassination was not such bad news for the firm?"

His voice turned almost falsetto.

"I beg your pardon! I did not imply anything of the kind! Please don't misunderstand me."

I copied the addresses of the children in question.

"Will Mrs. Böllig take over as director of the firm?"

"No decision has been made about that. During the transition period, I am in charge."

There was pride in that statement. He must have been

seeing himself in that position for quite a while. I wondered how well he was getting along with the widow. Rich, decadent, and lazy, she was bound to irritate the ambitious Meyer. I got up.

"Many thanks, Mr. Meyer. I hope I haven't taken up too much of your time."

We shook hands, and I walked through the door. The princess was smoking, waiting for Meyer. She looked at me anxiously as I walked past her. I proceeded down the dark, empty hallways, in the throes of a nicotine fit.

▪5▪

It was half past six. I passed through the foyer and crunched across the wet gravel to my car. The road was lit by yellow fluorescent lights. Fifty meters to the left stood the firm's refreshment kiosk. Its red neon lottery sign flickered restlessly. I walked over and knocked on the window. Through the rain-splattered pane I saw a small figure approaching with a limp, like an old boat in rough seas. She squinted hesitantly through the window before she slid it aside.

"What is it?"

This female Hunchback of Notre-Dame was only a little taller than the counter. It occurred to me that people might set their beers down on her head, by mistake. Her nose was running, and her chin and upper lip were covered with an unruly, goatlike beard. She had a hard time looking up at me. I put a twenty-mark note in the tray.

"Two packs of Luckies and an Asbach."

Her crooked fingers took the money and shoved it

under the counter. Then she limped over to the cigarette shelf and then to the other, the cookie and alcohol shelf. It took a while, but she found everything. She rummaged in the cash box and pushed my change across the counter. Through the open door in the back I caught a glimpse of an old iron bedstead.

"Do you live here?"

"None of your business."

"It was just a question. Maybe you heard something, the night of the attack."

"I heard the big bang. Like everybody else."

"No gunshots?"

"Oh yes."

"When did you hear those?"

"Before the bang."

"*Before* the bang?"

"Yes. So?"

"How much time passed between the shots and the big bang?"

"I don't know. I don't have a watch."

"Five minutes, half an hour, an hour?"

"Ten minutes."

"Are you sure?"

"Is that all you want? I closed up quite a while ago."

She started sliding the window shut.

"Did you know Mr. Böllig?"

The window had a couple of centimeters to go. She hesitated. "Yes. You could say I did."

The window closed. Her shadow receded slowly through the door in the rear. I lit a cigarette, sipped some Asbach, and trotted back to Riebl's Rabbit. A Renault Five was parked right behind it. I got into the Rabbit and drove down to the main road. Just before the entry ramp to the freeway, I noticed the Renault right behind me. I slowed down to take a look. The driver was alone in the car. On the freeway, I passed four trucks, swooped back into the right lane, and slowed down to eighty. The Renault zoomed past me on the left. I speeded up and caught up with it. It was crawling along at seventy. I had hardly passed when it picked up speed again and stayed on my tail. I changed tactics and tested the Rabbit's top speed. At a hundred and seventy, I visualized Riebl's face if I brought his car back minus its doors. I slowed down to a hundred and thirty and tried to ignore the headlights of the Renault.

At the Frankfurt West Exit, I turned toward the trade fair buildings. I knew of a dead-end street near there. The Renault stayed with me as unobtrusively as a police escort. The driver was either a pro who wanted to scare me, or else an amateur. I charged down the street at seventy, slowed down at the corner, and made a sharp left turn. When I saw the Renault come around with similar bravado, I accelerated briefly and then braked to a complete stop. The pavement was wet and covered with slippery leaves. I skidded to the right and stopped at right angles to the street. My pursuer slammed on the brakes and came to a screeching halt, banging into the driver's side door. I scrambled over the passenger seat and out into the street, ran around the Renault, and yanked the driver's door open.

"Hey, what a surprise!"

Carla Reedermann stared at her knees. I grabbed her arm and pulled her out of the car.

"Now let's hear what you have to say."

She tried to wriggle out of my grip, and when I didn't let go, she started yelling.

"Let me go, you asshole! Take your paws off me, you ..."

I slapped her.

"Calm down. Not everybody knows how to play detective ... You were doing that this morning, at the courthouse! You knew that Anastas wanted to hire me. Then there was all that playacting in the wine bar ... your moon-faced friend thought he was being clever, faking surprise—'What, you two know each other?' I don't mind if people feel like acting like idiots. But I do get bothered having the same set of headlights in my mirror."

I let her go and lit a cigarette. She rubbed her wrists. After a while she opened her mouth.

"I—all right, you're right, but—"

"But?"

She raised her head.

"You have no idea what's at stake in this case!"

"No? I don't?"

"No! If you had an idea, you wouldn't have acted so cool this morning. Do you know how many people were pleased that Böllig was killed by Greens? Not because he was a competitor—his little firm is quite insignificant—but because the chemical industry had found its martyr. And it needed one. Lately people have become altogether too interested in the environment. There are increasingly massive demands for measures to protect it—just think about the Rhein Main plant. Everybody was against its relocation in Vogelsberg. Now, after Böllig, it can be built there. And do you know who's a shareholder in Rhein Main Farben? The Mayor of Frankfurt. That's news to you, isn't it?"

"And how. They don't write about stuff like that in the sports pages."

For a moment she looked confused.

"So you see who is interested in having those four convicted without any more ifs and buts! We wanted to know if we could trust you. I have no experience with private investigators. We need someone who is on our side. For all we knew, you might have been in cahoots with the police. Checking us out for them. That would have been the end, for us. What do we know about you? True, you once got three police officers thrown into jail, but that may not mean all that much. I'm helping Anastas with the case, and it was my idea to test you first."

"By totaling my car?"

"I'm sorry. I never tailed anyone before. And you didn't have to slam on the brakes."

"I see. And what results did you expect?"

"Maybe you would have driven directly to the police ... or something. And besides ..."

"Yes?"

"All right, I wanted to find out more about you. We hardly know one another, and yet we're supposed to collaborate in such an important case. You haven't told me anything about yourself. I'd like to know where you live, what else you do. And you're a Turk. That's a different culture, and we may not be able to communicate ... Perhaps it was foolish, but I didn't want any surprises. For instance—whether you would accept a woman as a co-worker. I mean, that's unusual where you come from, isn't it? Do you see what I mean?"

I stared down the wet street and considered dropping the case.

"I don't have the faintest idea."

She looked lost. I walked slowly to my car.

"My job is to get four people out of jail. If the murderer is still at large, I'll find him. Maybe I'll ask you to brew me a cup of coffee one of these days. Maybe not. I'll just do my job. I'll see you at eight, at Anastas's place."

I slid across the passenger seat, started the engine, and steered the car slowly past the Renault. I stopped briefly next to Carla Reedermann and leaned out of the window.

"Besides, it isn't the mayor who holds those shares. It's his wife." I drove off. I could still see her in the rearview mirror. Her dark hair shimmered under the streetlights.

Riebl gazed sadly at the dent.

"I'm sorry, Mr. Riebl. It was slick. Someone skidded into me."

I gave him Anastas's address, telling him to collect there.

"Anytime you lend anything to anybody ..."

He ran his fingers gently over the dent. I walked over to my Opel. Once again, Riebl had managed to fix it. Two blocks down the street I parked and went into a restaurant. It was ten minutes to eight. Three large guys sat in a corner, playing skat.

The proprietor brought me a plate of ribs with sauerkraut. One of the skat players went to the jukebox and played "Ninety-nine Balloons." I have never been able to figure out the words. The proprietor coughed and hummed along.

A short while later I got up and paid.

"Say, Fritz, since when do you serve guys like him?"

One of the drunken cardplayers gave me a challenging stare.

"No politics," growled the proprietor.

I turned and went out. Maybe I should have tossed his glass of schnapps in his face.

Anastas's office was in a stylishly renovated old building. I walked up the red-carpeted stairs to the second floor. Anastas stood in the doorway, smiled, shook my hand.

"I was afraid you weren't coming."

"Why?"

"Miss Reedermann told me about your encounter."

"Encounter is funny."

He led the way to his office through a mirrored entrance hall. Several stacks of files covered his desk, in front of which stood four worn leather armchairs. Except for one cheap lithograph, the walls were bare and white. Carla Reedermann stood leaning against a radiator, perusing the daily papers. She looked up briefly and gave me a nod. Anastas asked, "Coffee, beer, wine—what would you like?"

"I'll take a beer."

While he went to get it, I stared out the window.

"That Rabbit I was driving belongs to the owner of my auto repair shop. I gave him Anastas's address. Is that OK?"

"Uh-huh."

The little lawyer returned, handed me a glass and a bottle of beer, and sat down on the edge of his desk, his legs dangling.

"Now, Mr. Kayankaya, I have to apologize, and then I have to explain a few things to you."

He folded his hands solemnly. I sipped my beer and listened to things I already knew. Then he cleared his throat and looked at me expectantly. Carla Reedermann was also watching me, her eyelids lowered.

"Have you found the camping enthusiast and his friend?"

A brief pause.

"Oh, I see, ha, ha ..." His laugh sounded silly. "Mr. Kayankaya, I'm so glad you've decided to stay with the case."

He jumped down off the desk and shook my hand again. After he had calmed down and seated himself behind the desk, even Carla Reedermann granted me a smile. I asked myself if anyone except for me was at all interested in who had shot Böllig, and whether Anastas's clients didn't deserve their time behind bars. I lit a cigarette.

"Well, is he coming here or isn't he?"

"He said he'd be here at nine o'clock."

"Good. Let me take a look at those files until then."

I went up to the desk, and Anastas explained the contents of the files. First I looked at the autopsy report. Four nine-millimeter bullets. Two in the stomach, one through a lung, one grazing the top of his head. Fired from a distance of circa ten meters. The assassin must have been a beginner, or else drunk out of his mind. Time of death, between midnight and half past. I copied the doctor's address, and went on to study the defendants' dossiers. All four of them were in their mid-twenties and had made an early start working for one cause or another in various groups, without attracting particular attention. One of them came from Doppenburg, the other three from Frankfurt. I copied their addresses. According to their statements, they had grown tired of handing out leaflets in vacant pedestrian malls, knowing that no one read them anyway. Then came the idea of a big bang to wake up the people, and they obtained explosives from a chemistry student. They refused to answer questions about the fifth man. When, on the morning after their act of sabotage, they heard about Böllig's murder, all of them wanted to leave the country and go to Greece. After prolonged discussion, they discarded that idea and waited for further developments. Three days later, the police arrived. They didn't look like killers to me.

"Another beer?"

"Yes, please. None of them gave a more detailed description of how they got the idea to blow up that pipe?"

"No."

"One of them must have thought of it first."

"They claim they developed the idea collectively."

"Developed the idea! Bullshit. I have to talk to them."

"They don't want to do that under any circumstances."

"Then think of something. You're the attorney. Put pressure on them. How am I supposed to get on with my job?"

"I'm sorry, Mr. Kayankaya, but I don't want to put any strain on my relationship with my clients. You must understand that."

"They're facing fifteen years in prison, and you're talking about relationships? Once they're convicted of murder, you'll have to find another outlet for your interpersonal horseshit ... How did the cops find out so quickly? Someone must have squealed. As soon as they realize that, they'll denounce that someone. If they don't, they're idiots. But if they aren't, and they still won't talk, I can stop playacting the clever detective. Because if that's the case, they *did* snuff Böllig. Makes sense, doesn't it?"

Anastas paced about with a furrowed brow.

"You may be right. Let me get you that beer."

I looked at Carla Reedermann.

"And what do *you* think we should do? Collect signatures? Print up a leaflet? How about a hunger strike? We could shackle Anastas to the courthouse fence for a week."

She smiled. It was a pretty smile.

The doorbell rang. A moment later, Anastas returned with a young man wearing jeans and a sports jacket, followed by a knock-kneed blonde with no ass. Both of them looked as if this was their first time away from home after nine in the evening. We shook hands, and Anastas made introductory remarks. Alf Düli and Anita Weiss had been engaged for a year and planned a wedding for next summer. Alf Düli was finishing his apprenticeship as a bank clerk. He guided his fiancée to the window, sat down in an armchair facing me, leaned forward, and beamed. I asked Anastas and Carla Reedermann to leave the room.

"On the night of the twenty-second of April, you put up a tent on the factory grounds of Böllig Chemicals?"

"*Next* to the factory grounds, not on them."

"All right. By the lake. Tell me what it was like."

Alf told me that his parents had discovered that lake a long time ago, opined that it was surely all right to spend a night together in a tent without a marriage certificate, and went on to explain how many cans of provisions they had been able to fit into his Rabbit. I interrupted him.

"Mr. Düli, what woke you up in the middle of the night?"

"The explosion, of course ..."

"Any gunshots?"

"Yes, of course."

"Before or after the explosion?"

"Ah ... More or less at the same time ... No, right after. Böllig came running *after* he heard the bang, didn't he?"

"I'm asking you if you heard any gunshots, and when you heard them. I'm not asking you for your conjectures."

"Well, I'm really not totally sure, but it stands to reason ..."

I turned to the little blonde.

"What about you?"

"I can't remember anything except for that explosion."

"But Anita—"

"Please! So, Ms. Anita, you heard no gunshots?"

"No. I didn't hear any."

"What did you do after you heard the explosion?"

Düli made a fist. "I grabbed my knife, and then I—"

"I'm talking to your friend."

His Boy Scout smile froze. He leaned back, clenched his jaw, and looked offended.

"Yes, Alf rushed out, and I followed, and we could just still see those four running away."

"Those four? Not five?"

"Oh yes, a little while later one more ran across the field."

I lit a cigarette.

"Could it be that one of the four had turned around, and that you just saw him twice?"

"If so, he must have been running damn fast."

"All right. And then?"

"We waited there, by the tent, for about fifteen minutes. Then the police came."

Düli couldn't stand it any longer. He demanded center stage.

"I wanted to go after them right away, see what they were up to. I knew they were up to no good. But Anita, you know how women are, she got scared, and so—"

"Yes, all right." I turned back to the girl. "Did they take statements from you?"

"They took our names and addresses, and the next day

we had to go to the station. Two weeks from now we have to appear in court as witnesses. That's all."

"Did you know the Böllig family?"

"No."

"That's all. Many thanks."

I got up and shook hands with them. Alf Düli demonstrated one more time what a guy he was by almost crushing my hand. I called for Anastas, and he escorted the couple to the door. Carla Reedermann came in and sat down on the edge of the desk. In her tight skirt, she did that really well. Her long legs swung gently. I watched her and pondered what kind of a test this might be.

"Did you find out anything?"

"Why do you ask? I'm sure you kept your ears glued to the door. Didn't you?" She stopped swinging her legs, shrugged. "We did."

I leafed through papers on the desk. Then Anastas came back and set a bottle of beer on the desk.

"You don't have anything on Böllig's private life?"

"Just the usual. Born, married to, and so forth. Why?"

"The most revealing thing about a murder is its motive. And the most revealing thing about a motive is the victim. It's as simple as that."

I finished my beer and took my leave, reassuring them that they would be hearing from me.

.7.

I parked by the fence and walked over to number five. A wet wind swept down the street and struck my neck like a spray of cold water. Number five was a building from the fifties with a fluted glass door. I rang the bell and waited. Heinzel, Lechmann, and Schmidi. Heinzel and Lechmann and their two buddies were now behind bars, tending their relationship with their attorney Anastas. That left Schmidi, if he was home. The buzzer sounded, and I pushed the door open. Schmidi stood in a doorway, in T-shirt and underpants. He was overweight but not obese; still, his thighs certainly did not indicate a macrobiotic diet.

I wished him a good evening, and he responded but did not budge from the door.

"What's up?"

"Kayankaya. I work for Dr. Anastas."

He scratched his hairy belly and scrutinized me.

"The lawyer?"

"Right. Can you spare a moment for a couple of questions?"

"... Awlright."

He took me to the kitchen, through a short hallway plastered with posters and newspaper clippings. A tattered Japanese paper lampshade lit the room. You could smell the garbage. I sat down at a table that looked homemade and watched Schmidi pick up some empty coffee cups. Then he leaned against the sink and stuck both his thumbs into the elastic of his underpants.

"Go ahead."

"Were you and Lechmann and Heinzel close?"

"What's that supposed to mean?"

"All kinds of things. For instance—have you given any thought to the Böllig case?"

He rubbed his unshaven chin.

"Well, what do you think? We've been sharing this place for two years."

"And why do you think those four were arrested so quickly?"

"Didn't surprise me. Computers and networks and all that shit. Of course it wouldn't take them long."

"Were you there when they planned the operation?"

"Oh no, boss. I didn't know anything about it, and all I know now is what I've read in the papers." He sneered.

"You're not a cop, are you?"

"Do I look like one?"

"Well, you guys were raised in a dictatorship ..."

He grinned. He liked his joke. I lit a cigarette and waited. "Has it occurred to you that the fifth man could have been an informer who ratted on his buddies?"

He leaned forward, made a serious face, and said, "You speak in riddles, chief. I don't know what you mean by the fifth man."

"It was in all the papers. There were *five* people at Böllig's. One of them is still running around free. The computers don't seem to be catching up with him."

"You mean the story by that character who was camping out there? No one believes that."

"But I do. And I ask myself why the police found those four in only three days, and haven't been able to find the one guy in seven months. Then I ask myself, how is it possible that four people can deny, so convincingly, that they committed a murder which they clearly ..."

"OK, chief, I see what you're driving at. Not a chance. I have nothing to do with any of it, I don't know any fifth man, and I'm not the least bit interested."

He crossed his arms and looked me up and down. More down than up. He was about thirty-five, lived in a run-down apartment, and knew that his train had been and gone. It was obvious that he felt somewhat illegal because he knew the fifth man's name but did not divulge it, and he was proud of that, without having the faintest idea who it was he was protecting. He was the kind of guy who walks down the street with you and at some point, a tear glittering in his eye, points at a window and whispers, "That's where Ulrike Meinhof hid for a while."

I tossed my cigarette into a half-empty yogurt container and got up.

"If that's all you have to say, Schmidi ..."

"Mr. Schmidi. I don't call you rat-Turk."

"So that's what you wanted to get off your chest all this time?"

"You better leave while the going is good."

"Yes, I might just give in to the urge to beat the name of that fifth guy out of you."

He took a step toward me.

"Fuck off!"

He was too unappetizing. I left.

For about ten minutes I stood behind the fence and kept an eye on the front door of number five. Then it opened. Schmidi looked quickly up and down the street, then walked off. It was raining again. I pulled my coat collar up higher and followed him. We made a left turn, then a right, then proceeded down an alley and ended up in front of Lina's Cellar. After scanning the street again, Schmidi went in. Five minutes later I followed. Lina's Cellar was a rustic tavern with a bulletin board next to the restrooms and a blonde behind the counter. I sat down at a vacant table and ordered some Scotch. The joint was fairly busy. I couldn't see Schmidi anywhere. A young couple next to me were frozen in rapt contemplation of each other's face and letting their plates of spaghetti get cold. Across the room, a group of young people were celebrating the end of a South American folk dance class. The waitress brought my Scotch and nodded in the direction of the celebrants. "They've been at it all night. One of them told me they're social-work teachers, and they'll be going to Nicaragua next. I bet those folks will be pleased to see them ..."

I grunted noncommittally. She crossed her arms and stared at the group.

I knocked back my Scotch and asked her to bring me another.

"Do you know what the French say when they see one of those painted VW buses?" she asked me when she came back. " 'Fritz is wearing camouflage again.' "

"Do you have a phone?" I asked.

"Through the door next to the restrooms and down the hall. It's on the left."

"Is there another exit?"

She smiled. "We don't get raided every week."

"I'm looking for someone."

I described Schmidi to her. She nodded and mumbled something that sounded like "barfly Guevara." "He came in a little while ago. You see those guys over there?" She nodded in the direction of three palefaces all in black. "They call themselves the 'Gallus Column' and spend their time drinking applejack. Schmidi is their guru. When he's had a skinful, he talks about the revolutionary avant-garde."

She checked me out.

"Why are you looking for him?"

"He knows someone I have to talk to."

She narrowed her eyes skeptically.

"You don't look like a cop."

"Nor am I one."

"I don't care. I have nothing to hide. I can tell any cop to take a hike."

She leaned forward. "Would you like another one?"

I nodded, but before she could pick up my glass, Schmidi's unshaven face appeared in the door next to the restrooms. He scanned the tables and fixed his gaze on me. For a second, our eyes held. The waitress understood and made herself scarce. Schmidi walked over.

"You're following me around?"

"What gives you that idea?"

He lit a cigarette, let the smoke trickle through his nostrils, and asked, "Who are you?"

"I'm a private investigator."

"A private investigator. Fancy that."

He grinned wearily.

"And you work for the lawyer?"

"That's right."

He let the cigarette dangle from his lips and put his hands in his pockets. He stood there for a while. I took the initiative. "Who did you call?"

"My true love, chief," he whispered, and grinned again. Finally he took the cigarette out of his mouth, stubbed it in the ashtray, and leaned across the table.

"All right, smartass. Maybe I do have something to tell you." With a glance to the counter, "But not here. Wait for me outside."

He turned and walked over to the palefaces. While I paid for my drinks at the counter, he left the joint. The waitress gave me my change and said, "I couldn't swear to it, but I think Schmidi's avant-garde is interested in you."

In the mirror above the bar I could see the three sitting there, motionless, staring at me. I found Schmidi leaning against a streetlight by the corner. It was pouring, his hair was soaking wet. He wiped his face with the back of his hand and said, "Let's take a little walk."

"Because it's such nice weather?"

"Because I don't want anyone to eavesdrop on us."

In silence, we trudged through the puddles in the direction of the Westbahnhof.

"There doesn't seem to be a whole lot to eavesdrop on."

Without looking at me, he muttered, "Give me a little time, man. I have to figure it out." He spat. "Besides, I have a photograph that might interest you. Don't want to pull it out in this rain. But there's this pedestrian underpass, a little ways ahead."

I didn't believe him about the photo, nor did I believe that he really wanted to tell me anything. But something was bound to happen. We turned into a narrow street and descended some steps to the underpass. Its walls were covered with all kinds of slogans, it was poorly lit, and it stank of urine. A shopping cart lay on its side by a wall. Our footsteps echoed. I stopped.

"Here we are, in your underpass."

We looked at each other. He put a cigarette in his mouth and nodded. People appeared at the other end of the passage. Three of them. Three palefaces. Schmidi grinned, cigarette between his lips, and said, "A light?"

I punched him and ran.

I charged up the steps, vaulted over a railing, slipped, rolled, got back up, and ran down the street. They were right behind me. I thought of the Beretta, safe between my underwear in the closet. The street forked, and I went left. A dead end, with residential buildings on both sides. I ran to a front door and grabbed the door handle. Locked, just as it should be. Before I could ring the bell, they were on top of me. Panting, they dragged me back to the side-walk and slammed me against a lamp post. Schmidi hissed between clenched teeth, "So now, you fucking pig ..."

He pulled my coat collar up while the other three hung on to my sleeves. They wrapped me around the post like a rubber band. Then one of them said, "He's a Turk, right?"

"But he's a cop, nevertheless."

He put his fist under my chin. "Still acting cool, hey, pig?"

"Tell your kiddies I don't need longer arms."

He swung and slapped me in the face with his open palm.

"You're just an asshole. Just like us. But the difference is that you've sold yourself to the pigs. You understand?"

"No."

"You're a Turk, all right, that's a bonus. A dago ... But if you try to sell us to the cops, we won't be so tolerant any-more. Is that clear?"

"Listen, man, I'm too old for your party."

He slapped me again, then held his index finger under my nose. "For the last time: I don't know anything about the Böllig affair, and I don't know the fifth man. And something else: you won't come snooping around again. Got it?"

The three were hanging off of me like shopping bags. I had had enough.

"If the fifth man isn't an informer, I'll buy you a soft drink."

His fist flew through the air, a white lightning bolt flashed through my skull, then everything turned gray. I tried to defend myself, but they hung on and pummeled me.

"Fucking traitor!" Then I was down on the sidewalk, and I stopped trying to ward off their blows. It was pointless. I saw their faces whirl above me like a carousel. A punch in the stomach, a kick to the head, fireworks, and curtains.

I woke to stinging pain. I opened my eyes and saw a crumpled Coke can. They had left me lying in the gutter. My head throbbed wildly. My tongue tasted blood. Something tugged on my pants leg, then crawled over it, and then there was that vicious sting again, in my arm. I rolled sideways and felt the wet fur, heard it squeak. A rat was hanging on to my arm and staring at me with its pinpoint eyes. I scrambled to my feet and pounded the rat, shouting, but it only tightened its jaws harder on my broken skin and flesh. Crazed with pain and revulsion, I made it to the next streetlight and slammed my arm and the rat against the pole. If the beast hadn't borne the brunt of the blow, I would have broken my arm. I banged it against the lamp post one more time and it let go, slid to the sidewalk, and ran squealing into the nearest storm drain. I leaned against the post, totally confused. The rat had torn my jacket and shirt, and I could see a mess of blood and broken skin. I was in urgent need of a doctor. Behind me, a front door opened, footsteps approached. "Good God! What happened to you?"

"Call an ambulance! Please!"

Then I blacked out again. When I came to, a man in a white coat was supporting me. We were still by the streetlight, but a crowd had gathered. Someone wanted to know what had happened. He was attacked by a rat, someone said. People giggled.

"Wow, that's wild, a Turk chewed up by a rat!"

Boom, boom, boom. That was my arm. A distant murmur reached my ears. My mouth tasted as if I had been sucking on a rotten herring. The murmur came closer and turned into a voice right next to me. It hurt my head.

"God, I hate the emergency room! Stabbings, alcohol poisoning, broken noses—it's always the same. This one's lucky to keep his arm. God, the garbage we have to deal with here at night! I used to feel pity, but now it's simply disgusting. When he wakes up, send him home to bed, and tell him how many of these pills he should take. If he doesn't understand, draw a picture."

"All right, doctor."

I squinted into the blinding white light. Slowly the white coats acquired outlines. I dragged myself up onto my right elbow. My left arm dangled lifelessly. Two men stood watching me the way anglers look at a poisoned fish.

"See you later, Heckler."

I raised my hand and croaked, "Doctor—"

He didn't turn around, just kept on going. Heckler was studying papers. I touched my damaged arm, moved its elbow and fingers a little. It was far from functional. It had always been the weaker arm.

"Heckler."

He didn't look up but indicated that I had his attention, growling, "Yes?"

"How is my arm?"

He put the papers aside and came to the cot. A young paramedic, clean-shaven, impeccably manicured, white clogs on his feet. Legs apart, knees straight, he stood before me.

"Not so hot." He clicked his tongue. "You should take better care next time."

"I want to know how my arm is."

He crossed his arms and rocked back on the wooden soles of his clogs.

"You have light to medium contusions all over your body and a laceration on your right leg. Your left arm is badly infected. We sewed it up as well as we could."

As he was speaking, he was performing a kind of mime.

"What do you mean, as well as you could?" I asked, after explaining to him that the laceration was on my leg and not in my brain.

"You'll have a scar, but," he smiled, "you won't think that's such a tragedy, will you?"

Was he implying that I wasn't photographic model material, anyway? I told him to go to hell and tried to get off the cot. I slid and dragged myself over to the chair with my clothes on it. They reeked of alcohol.

"Why does everything smell like that?" I asked.

"We disinfected everything."

I put on my shoes and reeled into the hall. Heckler clip-clopped along by my side. "Come back in two days, or have your own doctor take over."

I gave him my doctor's address and said goodbye. It was two o'clock in the morning. The silent hallway was lit by yellow emergency lights. I fired up a cigarette, shuffled through the reception area, and flagged a taxi. The rain had stopped. You could even see the moon. But I was already fast asleep.

▪ DAY TWO ▪

▪ 1 ▪

A huge rat in a pair of briefs sat on the edge of the bed, making a fiery speech about the forests of Germany as it kept grabbing one of my feet—I had at least ten—and nibbling on it. Then I was crawling on my stumps down an endless tunnel, past men in white coats who were hooting and pointing at me. From the other end of the tunnel a fat woman approached carrying a ringing telephone. She set it down in front of me, I picked up the receiver and said "Hello?" but no one answered. But it kept ringing and getting louder and louder, and I kept picking up the receiver. Finally I woke up, bathed in cold sweat. Someone was leaning on my apartment door bell like a madman. I threw off the covers and dragged myself over to the closet. The Beretta felt comfortable in my hand. According to my watch, it was twenty past five. Who the devil could this be? I touched my left arm. It hardly hurt anymore. The doorbell started ringing again, and now they were banging on the door as well.

"Open up! Police!"

I switched on the light, turned the key, took the safety

off the Beretta, and opened the door. It was, indeed, the cops. Four of them. They faced me in a half-circle. One of them saluted casually and asked, "You're Kemal Kayankaya?"

"As it says on the door."

"Come with us."

I stuck the gun in the pocket of my robe and told him what time it was.

"I have a warrant to place you under temporary arrest," he rumbled, and showed me a piece of paper. "If you resist, I have to put the cuffs on you."

The fingers of the three others hovered nervously above their pistols. I surrendered, and half an hour later we were at the precinct.

The cell was no more than three square meters, with a light green plastic toilet in a corner. The walls were covered with obscene graffiti. Above me to the right a small ventilation fan whirred. There were no windows. It was a little after seven by my watch. Outside, the sun must have risen.

I lay on a narrow cot, humming popular tunes to myself. They had turned the lights on half an hour ago—bright lights, which penetrated closed eyelids. A cop had brought me a jug of tap water and told me that the superintendent was still busy. The light became unbearable, and I pulled the gray blanket over my head. My cigarettes were in my overcoat, and the cop who from time to time stuck his head through the door refused to get me any. When one of the clowns pulled me out of the squad car, my arm had started bleeding again. I turned to the wall and tried to sleep, but with no success. I could feel the throbbing of the wound in my brain. So I got up and walked two steps forward and two steps back, back and forth, back and forth. Then I started kicking the toilet at one end and banging the peephole window at the other. Less than two minutes later a head appeared.

"What are you trying to do?"

"I'm trying to stop smoking."

"Come again?"

"You see a cigarette anywhere?"

He closed the hatch. I heard him say, "Willi, the Truk is freaking out." I stepped up on the toilet seat and held the blanket up to the ventilation fan. Instantly the stiff fabric jammed the blades. I banged the window again. "What's the matter now?"

I pointed at the fan. "I'm suffocating."

He pushed past me and saw the blanket. "Listen here, you asshole, there's a bunch of buddies back there who aren't feeling so good because it's been a fucking long night, and they'd like nothing better than to work you over! So shut up and lie down, you won't regret it."

"I want to call my lawyer."

He gave me a pitying look. Then he roared, "You don't understand what I'm saying! You don't even know what a lawyer is, for God's sake, you goddamn camel driver!"

I grabbed his green uniform collar and pushed him up against the wall. "Now it's your turn to listen to me. I got out of the hospital at two o'clock this morning, and three hours later you guys pull me out of bed, rip the stitches out of my arm, and throw me in a cell that would make any normal person sick! I want to call my lawyer!"

I let him go and sat down on the cot. He took a deep breath. "Very well, dago. I'll tell the superintendent that you're ready for questioning." He checked the time. "We'll save the raiding party for another time. I'm off duty."

I growled something about how I didn't give a shit, I'd fight all the fucking cops, let them just come by, including the superintendent. He was gone. I ripped the blanket out of the fan and it started whirring again. Then I heard footsteps, and the door opened. Two of them came in, handcuffed me, and took me out of the cell without a word. Our footsteps echoed in the long hallway. They stopped by a wooden bench and told me to sit down. After an eternity of ten minutes, they pulled me to the door facing the bench and into an office.

Behind the desk sat a nice little man with big ears. He looked at me as if he were in the market for a nice red balloon. I was planted in a chair facing him. The two uniformed cops left, and I was alone with the nice little man. He looked down at a piece of paper and read: "Kemal Kayankaya, private investigator. Born in Turkey. German citizen."

I nodded. He set the piece of paper aside and folded his hands.

"Four years ago I spent a week in Istanbul. An enchanting city. Truly enchanting. And the architecture! Of course," he lifted his palms in regret, "a little run-down. Not that you don't see that here too."

He scrutinized me kindly, fastened his gaze on the handcuffs, and exclaimed with feigned indignation, "These officers! Always so pedantic. They insisted on putting handcuffs on you. But I told them to treat you considerately." He shook his head. "Please, Mr. Kayankaya, you must forgive us. My staff is still so inexperienced."

Instead of removing the cuffs, he turned to look out the window, still smiling.

"I gather you have been complaining about the way they've been treating you?"

"I just wanted to speak to my lawyer."

"But you threatened an officer, didn't you? Do you realize you could be charged for that?" When he turned his eyes back to me, they were cold. "It's always the really clever ones who demand to speak to their lawyers right away. Are you a really clever one?"

He leaned back in his chair and rubbed one of his big ears.

"You're not answering me. Maybe you're a really stupid one?"

He chuckled, and laugh lines appeared around his eyes without softening them.

"Well, all right, let that go. You are presently investigating the Böllig case. That does not please me. I want you to resign from the job. If you refuse to do so, I'll ask for a warrant for complicity with the culprit and endangerment of our investigation. I don't want you to interfere in this case. It gives us the opportunity to uncover certain connections and organizations which we haven't been able to investigate until now. These things require delicacy and time. The police force does not consist only of idiots. We have been weaving a fine web, and you are about to tear it up, in all sorts of ways."

I rattled my handcuffs.

"Please take these off." He got up, put his hands in his pockets, and walked slowly around the desk.

"I've gathered some data on you, Kayankaya. You think you're a tough guy who can stick his nose into whatever he feels like."

"Is that all you found out?"

He sat down on the edge of the desk and folded his hands over his soccer-ball stomach.

"You're a boozer."

"Does that worry you?"

He picked up a metal ruler and pointed it at me. "What do folks drink in your parts? Raki, right? Would you like a shot?"

"No, thanks. I haven't had breakfast yet."

"A cigarette?"

I didn't reply. He reached across the desk and took a pack of Rothmans from a drawer. Unwrapping it, he asked, "So? You'll resign from the case?"

"I don't think so."

Furious, he tossed the pack in the wastebasket and came closer. I had had enough. I tried to get up, but he pushed me back into my seat.

"You stay where you are until we've settled this," he hissed at me through his teeth. Then he switched back to balloon man, smiled, and said in a low voice, like someone explaining the advantages of an account with their savings and loan association, "Listen carefully, Kayankaya ..."

He clasped his hand behind his back and strode slowly back and forth in the room.

"In here, I can beat you within an inch of your life, and no one gives a rat's ass. On the contrary, I may even get a pat on the back."

He studied his fingernails.

"Naturally, I prefer another solution. It wouldn't please me particularly to ... Well. Four officers would testify that you attacked me with a knife, and off you'd go to prison for attempted grievous bodily harm. But"—he beamed ecstatically—"things could get much worse." He patted my shoulder gently. "I could do things to your face, Kayankaya, that would make crashing through a windshield look like cosmetic surgery."

"You're really something, aren't you? You sit there like

a saint, relying on a bunch of uniformed hoodlums next door who are just waiting to have a little fun. Then you give me all this tough-guy shit."

He smiled.

"Mr. Kayankaya, do you really believe that I would call in my officers?" He laughed. "My, my, the ideas you get."

He giggled quietly as he walked back to the desk. He picked up the metal ruler, held it in both hands, and looked pensively at the floor.

"If you give me your word that you'll leave this case alone, I'll take those off"—he indicated the handcuffs, with his chin—"and you may leave. If you don't ..." He cleared his throat. "Well, then I'll be compelled to give my words a little additional emphasis."

For a moment he seemed to be lost in thought. Then he looked up and beamed at me. "You may rest assured that I am quite capable of taking care of things all by myself. To quite a satisfactory degree."

I told him that I was ready to believe in his abilities, but that it would only be fair if he took the cuffs off me first. After all, I said, I too had some talent for physical violence, and would be glad to show him a couple of tricks.

He giggled. "What a card you are."

Then he moved in close and placed the cold ruler under my chin. "So?"

There were only two choices. I picked the wrong one. I bounded off my chair and rammed both fists into his stomach, but I didn't hit him just right, and after he had reeled backward for a couple of meters, he was able to sidestep my second try, and I slammed into the desk. Before I could put my guard up, the ruler struck my ear like a red-hot iron bar, slid across my right cheek, and tore it. For several seconds, I became deaf. A fire raged in my head. Slowly the pain subsided. I looked up and saw him standing there, saying, "Tch, tch, tch ..." Then he took aim and hit me again, striking my wounded arm. I felt the hot sting. The wound broke open and spurted blood like a firehose. I fainted. When I came to again, the nice little man slapped me in the face. I closed my eyes. He slapped me again. I tried to crawl under the desk, but he caught my ankles by stepping on them. He stood there looking down at me, smiling.

"Now then, Mr. Kayankaya, have I been able to convince you?"

I wanted to tell him "convince" wasn't the right word, but only managed to spit blood. He took his heels off my ankles and sat down on the edge of the desk. "Get up. You're making a mess of my floor."

I pulled myself up. My cheek was throbbing. I dragged myself to the chair. The whole floor was smeared with blood. He came over and put his hand on my shoulder. "Just a little foretaste. But," he gave me a pat, "in two or three days you'll be fit as a fiddle again."

I closed my eyes. I heard a tap running. Then I received another slap in the face. "I'm sorry, but we aren't here to enjoy ourselves."

I held out my wrists. "Take these off and give me a cigarette."

He grabbed my hair and brought my face close to his. His eyes were like rocks, and he smelled of mouthwash.

"Kayankaya, I'm warning you. If you try to pull anything on me, I'll make you feel like this was a picnic!"

"Unlock these damn things!"

He let go of me. I fell back. Keys clinked, and he said, in a flutelike voice, "Get up."

I wrenched myself off the chair and raised my arms.

He grinned, and before I could duck, he slammed the bunch of keys into my face. I fell backward and banged into a bookshelf.

"You know what that's called in court? Resisting state authorities."

Then he unlocked the cuffs, and I felt a lit cigarette between my lips.

"And don't forget: This will remain our little secret. I trust you with that."

Then he sat down behind the desk and said quietly, but just loud enough for me to hear, "Kayankaya will no longer engage in any activities concerned with the Böllig case."

He wrote that in a small black book, put the book into a desk drawer, and went to the door.

"Hansmann!"

Hansmann, a fat blond with sloping shoulders, shuffled in.

"Get a rag and wipe up the mess."

He handed him the cuffs. "And rinse those off."

Hansmann grinned as if to indicate that his boss was the greatest, and disappeared. The boss approached me, holding out his hand, and said, "Well, Mr. Kayankaya, we have reached an agreement, haven't we?" In a sharper tone of voice: "I do hope you won't disappoint me."

He shook my hand, escorted me to the door as if I were his brother-in-law, and wished me a good day. I dragged myself through the hallway to the exit. On my way I passed Hansmann, who was carrying a bucket of water. Shaking her head, the girl at the switchboard watched us go our separate ways.

■ 2 ■

I was working on my third slice of ham on toast in the Hotel Intercontinental's breakfast room when Max Schwartz came marching in. He is a reliable fellow, and the boyfriend of one of the most beautiful women I know. Unfortunately, she is an alcoholic, and Max is also hitting the bottle, to drown his sorrows. He is a professional electrician and knows how to debug a room. He planted himself in a facing chair, squinted at me with interest, and said, "What on earth did they do to you?"

I gave him a brief report, adding that my doctor had brusquely shown me the door an hour ago after I had refused to take to my bed. Max looked around the large, impeccable room until he located the small group of waiters standing by the buffet and waiting for a soft clapping of hands. Max signaled to them and ordered coffee and Scotch. I abandoned my good intentions and did likewise. Around us, bankers took their seats. Young, tanned professionals, all of the same model, trim and fit. They ordered lox and champagne and appeared to be in excellent spirits.

I pondered what *I* would look like behind a desk in a bank. "So what's up?" asked Max.

I lit a cigarette.

"Yesterday afternoon I started looking into the Böllig case. Last night the cops came to get me and beat me up until I promised to leave well enough alone. I need to know who tipped them off—or if and how they managed to find out, all by themselves."

"You want to know if they bugged your office?"

"Not mine. The attorney's."

A little later, when the gentlemen next to us had elevated their mood with bubbly to the point of expounding and exchanging useful advice on the gliding capabilities of secretaries and prop planes, we paid and left.

A small señora in a brown smock, holding a bucket and a mop, came to the door. With many expressive gestures, she explained that she was Dr. Anastas's Spanish cleaning woman, and that he had not told her anything about our visit. After I too waved my arms a lot, to reassure her that I had recently joined Dr. Anastas's team, she allowed us to enter, albeit with some hesitation. Max started putting his equipment together in the entrance hall while I went in search of potables and found a refrigerator in the library. I returned with a bottle of champagne and three glasses. I had just poured them and persuaded the Spanish lady to have one when the phone rang. It was Anastas. I explained to him why I was there. He confirmed that my nice little man was a Detective Superintendent Kessler, and stated that he did not want any trouble with the police.

"You don't want any trouble with the cops, you don't want any trouble with your clients. You want me to spend my time playing ping-pong?"

He begged me to keep the lowest possible profile. "That's just great," I said, and hung up.

Max growled, "What kind of a guy is he, this attorney?"

"I really don't know. Some kind of a cross between Gandhi and a guy with a château in France. For presents, he gives his friends either bottles of wine or the works of Wallraff. I suspect that he is in favor of free elections in South Africa."

I lit a cigarette, drank champagne.

"How come he's defending those four?"

"So he can sleep at night."

"And why are you looking for the fifth man?"

"Probably for the same reason."

Next door, the señora's chamois squeaked against the windowpanes. Max sipped his champagne. "What happens if I find a bug?"

"Good question."

"Or if I don't?"

"If you don't, one of the people I met yesterday must have told the cops that I've entered the Böllig game. Someone known to Kessler. An informer."

Half an hour later, we were done. We were back in the car, and Max cranked the engine. Dense and heavy raindrops were falling from the sky and rattling on the roof. The window wiper on my side was out of commission. I couldn't see anything. Entering the traffic with caution, Max recapitulated. "So, as I told you, unless they've come up with something completely new, there are no bugs in that office. Maybe your attorney talked about it with someone in court, and the prosecutor's office passed it on to the cops? They're hand in glove, aren't they?"

"Maybe."

We stopped at a light. I looked at the window displays.

"Tell me, Max, do you know a joint called Lina's Cellar?"

"Leftist sort of place, with a touch of *bella Italia*. I've been there. Terrible wine, and the waitress wasn't so hot either."

"A buxom blonde?"

"That's right."

"Anything else you know about it?"

"They used to deal hash there. Now it's more the kind of place where male professors take their female students."

We stopped by my office, made a date to shoot some pool, and said goodbye.

"And how is Anna?"

He made a face.

"She's going into detox the day after tomorrow. So she's been really hitting the bottle for a week."

He turned and drove off. I entered the building and checked my mailbox. The Bilka store wished me a "good morning" and provided me with a lot of wonderful ideas to get shit-faced. Corn schnapps for seven marks, gin for twice that, and if nothing else worked, there was always the liter bottle of methylated spirits to really fry your liver. My office was on the third floor. It was cold and smelled of stale smoke. I turned up the heat and sat down at the desk. There was a dentist's office on the floor below me. For a while I listened to the faint hum of his drill. Then I picked up the phone book and found the number of *Rundblick* magazine. After three rings someone answered, and I asked to speak to Carla Reedermann.

"Reedermann speaking."

"Kayankaya. Could you please tell me exactly what you did yesterday?"

"Why—?"

"This morning the cops worked me over. Because of the Böllig case. I would like to know how they found out about me so quickly. Someone must have tipped them off."

"Are you implying that—?"

"I'm just wondering. First you show up at Anastas's, then you drive to Doppenburg, then there's all that talk about the female and cultural perspective ... Not too convincing. But look at it this way: You suggest to Anastas that I might provide a lead for the cops, and then you could keep tabs on me. Then, of course, the cops want to know what I have to do with the case."

Her breathing sounded labored. Typewriters were clattering in the background.

"So what now? You won't believe anything I tell you."

"Doesn't matter anyway. I promised Kessler to drop the case. In return, he told me who tipped him off."

"Wha-at?"

While she damned both me and the detective superintendent to the lowest pit of hell, and shouted that this was the worst swindle she'd ever been involved in, I retrieved my half-empty bottle of Chivas from a drawer, jammed the receiver between ear and shoulder, rinsed a coffee cup, and poured myself a drink. When she turned down the volume and her imprecations became more sporadic, I growled, "All right. Calm down. Kessler didn't tell me anything." Peace and quiet reigned for about a second, followed by a hoarse "What?" and another tirade. Screaming women give me a headache, unless they're screaming in Italian, and I hung up.

I took a pencil and a sheet of paper and made a plan. Half an hour later I had a list of names and many question marks. I decided to visit the night watchman again. He had been the least talented liar of all.

■ 3 ■

The small half-timbered house was the most run-down in the street. The plaster was crumbling, the woodwork had not been painted for ages, and the flowerpots below the windows were empty. The curtains were closed. I rang the bell. Above me, someone coughed quietly. A window opened.

"Who is it?"

A head with short, tousled blond hair looked down at me. She was in her early sixties. Her green eyes were alert.

"Is this the Scheigel residence?"

"What do you want?"

Her voice was gravelly from alcohol and cigarettes.

"I'm working for the public prosecutor's office on the Böllig case. Yesterday I talked to Mr. Scheigel, and I've come up with a couple more questions I'd like to ask him."

"Just a moment."

She closed the window. A moment later the front door opened.

"Please come in."

She wore a faded pink robe that must have been very expensive when it was new, a pair of slippers with heels, and a lot of rings and bracelets. I couldn't tell if the latter were genuine or not. Deep, dark lines underscored her eyes, and her cheeks were pale and puffy. A used-up face that still betrayed its former beauty.

She led me through a dark hallway to a kind of salon and told me to have a seat. The room was furnished with delicate pieces from another era. A heavy chandelier hung from the ceiling, and the place smelled of stale cologne. Here too the curtains were closed, and the faint daylight coming through them created a murky chiaroscuro. I sat down on the couch and watched her light a candle. Then she reached into a pocket of her robe and pulled out a pack of Russian cigarettes with paper mouthpieces. She took one, creased the mouthpiece, and stuck it into a gold cigarette holder. I lit it for her, and she sat down in an armchair.

"What is it you want to ask my husband?"

"I want to know why he didn't see a doctor after someone whacked him on the head."

She looked at me through the smoke of her cigarette.

"You don't work for the prosecutor's office."

"I don't? Why not?"

"Because." She smiled. "I like liars. They're romantic."

"I'm a private investigator."

"Well, there you are." She got up and took a bottle of vodka off a shelf. She got some ice from the kitchen.

"Would you like a drink?"

I nodded. She filled two hand-made crystal glasses and said, "Cheers."

It tasted better than any vodka I had ever had. I told her so. She laughed.

"It's genuine Russian. Contraband."

On the wall there was a brown photograph of a small girl with long braids. She was dancing on a dining table for an audience of adults.

"You were raised in Russia?"

"Poland. Warsaw. But that's a long time ago. When I've had a few more drinks, you can tell by my accent."

I liked her matter-of-fact attitude toward drink.

"And what brought you to Doppenburg?"

"Men. What else?"

We finished our drinks, and she refilled our glasses.

"Have you been living here long?"

"Half a lifetime. Back then, you took what you could get. Now it's too late. Here I am, and here I'll stay."

A convulsive cough shook her whole body. She apologized.

"It is horrible to get old. Old people can't walk too well anymore, they drool and smack their lips when they eat, they spit and cough ... Oh, how I hate it." She drank deeply from her glass. "All right, that's better."

I tried to think of a question to take her mind off her cough and her age. Finally I decided to ask her when she had first met her husband. He was, after all, the object of my visit.

"You really want to know?"

I nodded.

"Don't ask old people about their lives. Their memory is their life, and the less there was to it, the more they have to tell."

I said that nevertheless I was interested in her story.

She smiled. "But I have to start from the beginning. It's no fun for me otherwise."

She poured us another round and leaned back. Then, believe it or not, she told me her life story.

"In nineteen forty-five, I was seventeen years old. I left home at fifteen to make love to a German officer. Had I been older, I would have guessed that things wouldn't turn out well with that German, but I was young and thought I was betting on a winner. I hated my parents because they didn't like him, and were proud to be Poles. I wanted to get out of Warsaw. I wanted to see the world. America, China, Russia. I wanted to live. For me, Warsaw was too provincial, even though I had never been to a bigger city. I wanted to become famous, I dreamed of being a great dancer in Berlin. My parents insisted that I should enter an apprenticeship so I could take over the family tailoring business. Well, then the Russians came, my officer was shot dead, and I had to get by somehow. I was too proud to go back to my parents. Those were hard times. For a bag of potatoes, you'd do just about anything. The young Russian soldiers gave me enough to eat, and I entertained them at night. But even the Russians were poor, and their country was a shambles.

"A girlfriend and I decided to go west, to the Americans. We had heard you could really make some money there. A Polish fellow pawned his wife's jewelry, bought a car, and drove us the first hundred kilometers in the direction of Berlin. Unfortunately, every couple of kilometers he wanted to be rewarded. We got tired of him and took off. A Russian army patrol picked us up and took us to Berlin. They dropped us off in the American sector. There we realized that the pay wasn't much better than those old potatoes. The Americans were even worse about paying up than the Russians had been—maybe because their wives were still alive. But we did see our first genuine Negro, and we heard jazz. It was the world we had been looking for.

Then one day I met a dashing sergeant, the son of wealthy parents, and I thought this was my big break. I gave up my wicked ways and devoted myself to him. Days I would drink whiskey and mend his uniform, nights we would fantasize about a ranch in California. Unfortunately, I fell in love with him. I became sentimental and believed him when he said that the letters he received were from his sister. I didn't even notice his preparations for departure. He left me. I followed him to Cologne and Frankfurt, but finally he got on a plane to America, and I was back on the street. I didn't know anybody in Frankfurt, but it didn't take me long to get back into my old profession. I made a lot of money. In nineteen fifty-five I moved to Kronberg, where I worked only for regulars. That was a good time. I could afford everything I wanted, and things could have gone on like that ..."

She stuck another cigarette into her holder and inhaled deeply. Then she looked up.

"I warned you. It's been a long time since anyone shared my vodka with me. What's your name?"

"Kayankaya. Kemal Kayankaya."

"I thought so. You're not a German." She pointed to herself. "Nina Scheigel, née Kaszmarek." She laughed. She filled our glasses and continued her story. "Then one of those crazies showed up again, the kind that wanted to make an honest woman out of me. He was handsomer than the others, and he seemed more decent. He had a wife and children, but it was me he wanted. I was twenty-nine at the time, with another good ten years ahead of me. True, it would have been harder as time went on, and there comes a point when you have to pack it in. I didn't relish the prospect of walking the streets at forty. I accepted his offer. He bought a small apartment for me, here in Doppenburg, and paid me a decent monthly income. His wife knew about the arrangement. He came to see me almost every day. We took little trips, and I began to share his interest in books. I hadn't become a great dancer, but I had a carefree life. I did not love my patron, and it was better that way. The locals regarded me as a slut. Everybody knew.

"I used to have coffee with his wife, and at some point I got to know his son, a young man of nineteen. We took an instant shine to each other. For me, he was the hope of something new, and I started dreaming about America again. But one night his father caught us in bed together and kicked me out. He sent his son abroad. I followed him, and we had a wonderful time. When his father found out, he no longer sent money to the son, saying he wouldn't until I was out of the picture. For a while, we had a romantic time in fleabag hotels. But then he went back and entered the university, as his father wanted.

"I still had the apartment in Doppenburg, so I came back here and tried to forget the young man. I wasn't able to; I ended up spending more time drinking in the taverns than at home, not least because I would meet one of my lover's friends there. Fred Scheigel. I had first met him on the secret walks I took with my lover. Fred too was young and good-looking, and he had ambitions to leave and move far away from here. Just like me. We moved in together, and finally we got married. We never emigrated. Fred went to work. Then we opened a grocery store, but it didn't work. We went bankrupt and stopped dreaming.

"My lover returned to take over his father's business. He didn't want to have anything to do with me. Then his father suddenly died. He married another woman. And so I end up here, with an old idiot of a husband. The Polish slut. My social life consists of an old Russian in Frankfurt. He gets me this vodka. I'm fifty-eight, but I look ten years older, and I'll die in this hovel."

She got up for a fresh pack. Then she said, with a cigarette between her lips, "Six months ago, my lover was killed. I wanted to go to the funeral, but they didn't even let me see his grave."

Rain was drumming against the windows. It had grown dark, and I could see only her outline, and once in a while her face, in the glow of the tip of her cigarette.

"Böllig was your lover?"

She nodded. She lit another candle.

"And your husband worked for him as a night watchman."

She produced another bottle of vodka.

"You look like you have a good head for alcohol."

I held out my glass, and she filled it.

"Yes. Fred was out of work, and I wanted to help him. So I asked Friedrich Böllig to help him out, for old time's sake. He laughed and asked me why on earth I had shacked up with such a nonentity. It was repulsive, but he was right. He gave Fred a job as a night watchman. I cursed him for it, but I still loved him."

"Do you know his wife?"

"What do you think ... A young woman, after his money. She could have had the money, if she'd let me keep the man."

"Did he know that?"

"I don't know. The few times I saw him, I tried to make him understand, but he just got mad, yelled at me, called me names. He claimed that I had destroyed his relationship with his father, even accused me of having caused his death."

"What did his father die of?"

She stared at me for a moment. Then she leaned back in her chair and laughed.

"You think I killed him?"

"I don't think anything."

"Even if you did, who cares? Cause of death: circulatory collapse. Quite banal. He was overweight."

"Was his death convenient to anyone at the time?"

"I don't know that it was particularly *in*convenient, from anyone's point of view."

She got up and started pacing slowly back and forth across the room.

"Otto Böllig wasn't the type people grieve over. He was a tyrant, but not an intelligent one. He had no charm, he was a bore, almost a simpleton. Friedrich was something else. He was smart, witty, always ahead of the game. He was able to insult people and then placate them with a single gesture. He took them by storm. Besides, he was young, good-looking, and rich. He enjoyed life. For his father, the factory was everything—I think I was the only luxury he ever permitted himself in his whole life. Friedrich did well, until his father died. He was approaching thirty and realizing that charm and youth would soon be over. And there was this factory, and it wasn't in Munich or Düsseldorf, it was in Doppenburg, and someone had to run it. From then on, the factory became his life. At first he tried to keep up his old lifestyle: nights in Frankfurt or Cologne, days at the factory, but at some point he realized that the factory would lose out under this arrangement. And then he made the biggest mistake of his life. He married his nineteen-year-old secretary, believing that he could hold on to his youth that way! And she was a pretty little thing. Not only that—she knew exactly what she wanted."

She crossed her arms and looked at me.

"I don't say that out of jealousy. I admire women who have no illusions. But this girl was a champion of cunning. Friedrich had fallen in love with her, and he believed everything she said, just as I had once believed my American sergeant. She forced the philanderer to his knees. Somehow he then managed to convince himself that he had come out ahead in the deal. After all, he was a successful businessman with a pretty wife, and so on ..."

She laughed bitterly. It was time for me to ask a couple of questions. It was also time to admit to myself that I was drunk. I tried to marshal my thoughts, but didn't come up with anything better than "So you loved him until the end?" And the drama rolled on.

"Call me crazy, go ahead—but, yes. Even after he had turned into an evil person."

"What does that mean?"

"All kinds of things. Ask his mother what she thought of her son. She did not show up at his funeral."

"Oh, I didn't know ..."

"Yes. Herta Böllig, Otto Böllig's widow, is still alive. When you drive up to the plant, you'll pass a refreshment kiosk where an old woman sells cigarettes and beer."

The female Hunchback of Notre-Dame. Slowly I closed my mouth again. The Polish woman understood.

"So you've met her? Right. Soon after Friedrich got married to Brigitte, the latter decided that the old lady was an encumbrance to the household. Friedrich resisted at first, but she was soon relocated to an outbuilding that had been used as a storage space. Her next and final stop would have been the old folks' home. Without consulting anybody, Herta Böllig fired the man who was running the kiosk, furnished the back room, and moved in. You can imagine what a scandal that was, here in Doppenburg. Friedrich tried everything to get her out of there, but she wouldn't leave. Finally he let his wife convince him that it was the best arrangement for all concerned. People got used to it. Among the employees it became a taboo subject. I am the only person she still talks to. I, the former mistress of her husband."

Such a story, such vodka. God, the stories I would be able to tell when I was sixty ... But maybe I was more like one of those plays without a plot, I told myself; and besides, who would want to drop in on me?

"Now that we've opened this can of worms—tell me, what happened to Friedrich Böllig's son? I'm told he is in an institution?"

She had another hefty slug of vodka, leaned against the window bench, held her glass with both hands. Eastern Europeans have a special wooden leg for the stuff.

"That's all I know. I've never seen the child. He lives in a closed ward. Meningitis, right after he was born."

"You know the name of the institution?"

"Sorry, I don't even know the boy's name. All I know is that neither Friedrich nor his wife cared for him much. They've really buried him in silence. You are the first person in years who has asked me about him."

She walked out of the room, holding herself exaggeratedly erect. I heard the toilet flush. Then she returned with a bottle of mineral water. She put the vodka away. I drank three glasses of water in a row and felt more or less human again.

"Do you know a guy named Henry? An acquaintance of Brigitte Böllig's?"

"She has many acquaintances. I haven't paid any attention to their names."

A key turned in the front door. A moment later, Fred Scheigel padded into the salon. His hair was wet, and he looked perplexed.

He cast a disapproving look at me, at his wife, at the glasses. He nodded and mumbled, "Good evening." She said, "Fred, you've met Mr. Kayankaya. He wants to know why you didn't go see a doctor about your head injury."

An amazing memory. I wouldn't have remembered why I had come here.

Fred Scheigel slowly divested himself of his overcoat and folded it carefully over the back of a chair.

"But I did explain that to him."

"I don't know if I'd call it an explanation. But I have

another question: Before you were attacked—did you hear gunshots?"

He got annoyed. "Questions, questions, always the same questions! I told the police everything!" He looked at me grimly. "I was out cold *before* the explosion!"

"The shots were fired before the explosion."

Both of them stared at me.

"But ..."

"There are witnesses."

The Polish woman closed her eyes and did some quick thinking.

"But what was Friedrich Böllig doing down by the waste pipes, in the middle of the night?"

"I've asked myself that. What do you think, Mr. Scheigel? Did your boss sometimes patrol the grounds, check up on things?"

He hesitated. "Once in a while, I suppose." After a pause: "Quite regularly, really. He would drop by the cabin to see me."

His wife gave him a suspicious look. I couldn't tell whether I or the presence of his wife embarrassed him. I would have liked to talk to him alone. But I couldn't do that now. It was after six o'clock, and I had found out enough for one afternoon.

"It's getting late, and I ..." I looked at Scheigel and asked him without warning, "You didn't happen to call the police about the conversation we had yesterday?"

He looked surprised, shook his head.

"No, I didn't."

Heavy with vodka, I rose cautiously off the couch and tried life in the vertical position. It felt precarious, but I managed.

"About your vodka, madam—is it available only to fellow Slavs?" I did not want this to be a once-in-a-lifetime experience. She smiled.

"I'll give you the address."

While she was out of the room, I handed Scheigel my card.

"Just in case. You can call me any hour of the day or night. Should you feel like it."

Hesitantly he looked at the card, then at me.

"Your story is lame. You know that as well as I do. Sooner or later, you'll be found out."

His wife came back, and he slipped the card into his pants pocket.

"Here—I wrote a few words of recommendation on it. Nikolai is a sweet person, but don't let him overcharge you. He likes to exaggerate."

I thanked her, and she walked me to the door. Scheigel stayed in the salon, after shaking my hand without meeting my gaze. I took my leave of the Polish woman.

"Until next time."

She ran her fingers through her tousled hair.

"You want to hear more of my blather?"

I laughed.

"Oh, get going, young man."

I walked down the cobbled street. At the corner I turned to look back. The pink robe had disappeared.

■ **4** ■

The door was ajar. It was quiet. A little too quiet. I pushed the door slowly open with my foot. The three large mirrors that had adorned the entrance hall to the right and to the left now lay distributed in shards all over the pale carpet. I tiptoed to the office, toward the quiet whimpering I could hear coming from it. I entered and almost tripped over a broken chair. The desk had been overturned, three of its legs sticking up in the air, the fourth lying in the chaos of desk drawers, books, and all kinds of documents. The leather armchairs had been slit open. The stuffing swelled out of the gashes. The papers rustled in the draft coming from the broken window-panes. Someone had spray-painted large black letters on the wall: ACTION COMMANDO FREEDOM AND NATURE.

I waded through the debris to the whimpering closet. It was locked, and there was no key. I kicked the lock, and my foot crashed through the closet door. I could hear Anastas squealing. I managed to break down the door. Behind it, Anastas lay folded into the narrow space like a fat baby. His hands had been tied with his necktie and his nose was bleeding, a result of my kicking in the door. He had been blindfolded with a kitchen towel. I unknotted it and the necktie, helped him to his shaky legs, and put him in a chair. He leaned back and closed his eyes.

As far as I could tell, he wasn't seriously injured. No black eyes or missing teeth, not to mention unnaturally dangling arms. His nosebleed had stopped. His cheeks were red and swollen, though, and he had lost the buttons on his shirt. It looked as if he had been slapped around. The room was freezing. I stuck pieces of cardboard in the broken window, turned up the heat, and went to look for a calorific drink. When I came back with a half-full bottle of Rémy Martin, Anastas was crawling through the debris, looking for something.

"Here, have a hit, it'll do you good."

He looked at the bottle as if it were poison and said plaintively, "No, no thanks."

"If not, not," I said to myself, tilted the bottle for a hearty slug on his behalf, and reclined in an armchair until I realized that Anastas was crawling around looking for his glasses. I found them for him, under the radiator. The right lens was broken. He put them on and surveyed what was left of his office. Then he took a deep breath, took the bottle out of my hand, and knocked back at least a centimeter.

"Smoke?"

He nodded. After a couple of puffs, he said, "I thought I'd die in that closet."

"A few slaps won't kill you."

He looked at me grimly.

"They won't? You smartass. What about all this?"

He leaned toward me and yelled, "They beat me up! They tortured me!"

"And who were *they*?"

"Who! My clients, their friends, their sympathizers— what do I know. Just look at this!"

He gestured grandly at the chaos. I took the brandy back and returned to my chair while he went on ranting.

"And to be honest with you, it's your fault! It happened because of *you*. Why do you think they came here? To tell me to fire you! Let me tell you, I'll pay you what I owe, right now, and that'll be the end of our collaboration. I'm not a street fighter, I'm an attorney!"

I lit a cigarette.

"So that's news to you, isn't it? If only I had known, I—"

"Let's take it from the top. How many of them were there, and when did they get here? Pull yourself together."

He waved his arms in the air and shouted, "Pull myself together! I've just been assaulted, brutally, and you talk about pulling myself together! Put yourself in my place!"

He was gasping for air. When he seemed to have calmed down, I asked politely, "Well?"

He leaned against one of the legs of the desk and started talking, more to himself than to me.

"There were two of them. The doorbell rang around six thirty. I had been arranging books on my library shelves. I went to the door. Two men, all in black with pantyhose over their heads, grabbed me and dragged me into my office, beating me up as they went. It was pointless to resist, they would have killed me. One of them was at least two meters tall. A monster with huge shoulders, and he had a gun." He stopped, looked at me, and shouted, "I'd like to have seen what *you* could have done!"

I mumbled something and asked him to go on with the story, but he stayed on this sidetrack for a while, graphically describing how I would have fared, how I would have begged for mercy, and so on. He was quite imaginative. Somewhere along the line he lost the thread and fell silent.

"Did those two say who or what they were?"

"You've seen it. Action Commando 'Freedom and Nature.'"

"Right. But what's that supposed to mean?"

"Supposed to mean, supposed to mean! How would I know what that's supposed to mean? They said they were comrades of the ecological front, united in the struggle for life and nature. So you see, Böllig, the lake, clean water—it all fits."

I got up and gave him a little pat. "Mr. Anastas, that's a bad joke. 'Freedom and Nature.' I can't believe that your clients' friends would parody themselves like that."

"You just know that, don't you."

I rounded on him and shouted, "Yes, I do, I fucking well do know it! And I know a few other things too! I know practically everything! And if you don't stop acting out, I'll see to it that you start feeling homesick for those two playmates of yours. Now then: Why did those thugs make such a mess of everything?"

He cleared his throat, looked cowed.

"All right ... if you have to know. They accused me of having hired a cop." He avoided my eyes. "They said I was a traitor, not worthy of defending their friends in court, and so on. Believe me, they meant it too. While I tried to explain, they busted up my office. They had tied me up, so I couldn't do anything about it. Finally, after I promised to dismiss you, they locked me in the closet." He reverted to the complaining mode. "Why me? Why didn't they visit you? It would have made more sense. To victimize me, after all I've done for those people."

He raised a fist. "But this does it. I'll pay them back."

"Whom?"

"Whom? Who has such friends, won't hesitate to commit a murder. I've realized that I am not defending innocent people."

"I see. You've realized that. Gosh, that's really sharp."

I turned away from him and strode back and forth.

"That's really great PR for your practice. Someone slaps you around a bit, and you drop your clients like hot potatoes."

"It's easy for you to talk big. Any one of my colleagues would give up a case under such conditions."

"Time for me to go, then. And that'll be four hundred marks."

For a moment he looked as if he wanted to protest, but then he found his checkbook, wrote the check, and handed it to me. "Scared?" I asked him. He waved his arms.

"Of course I'm scared. They'll come back! They're a gang of murderers and bomb throwers. They'll kill me!"

"You better take very good care of yourself the next few days."

He looked flabbergasted. "What do you mean by that?"

"I don't believe this bullshit about 'Freedom and Nature.' I told you I'd find the fifth man, if he exists. So I'll go on looking. Since your clients were unlucky enough to get hold of such a wet blanket of a lawyer, they at least deserve a halfway decent detective."

He turned purple and snarled, "No, you won't! Because then they'll believe ... You have no right to do that!" He came toward me, pointing at me. "I'll inform the police! You are threatening my life, you're inciting the entire mob to go for my throat. I'll demand protection!"

I grinned. "You won't die. Guys like you don't die that easily. But you'll stay scared until this case has been solved. You'll stay scared even if they station half the guys in the precinct at your front door. What a hell of a guy you are."

I tapped my forehead and left. He followed me into the hall. "You'll leave the case alone, won't you? If I hadn't hired you, you would never have thought of ..."

I pulled the door shut behind me.

■ 5 ■

The windows were open onto the steady patter of rain. I was leaning my elbows on the desk in my office. The other agencies and physicians had all closed up shop, and I was alone in the building, except for the janitor watching television in his basement apartment. Scraps of music wafted from the Chicken Inn across the street. It was time to have my client chair reupholstered. My bottle of Chivas lay in the drawer. I tried to think about something else. Women. Once I knew a girl with whom I spent rainy days drinking tea and playing backgammon. Now and again, one of us would go out for cigarettes. In the evenings we lit candles and sipped champagne ... and so forth.

There was a water stain on my ceiling. The credit agency above me had installed a bathtub not too long ago. It was useful for keeping the beer cold, the cashier had told me.

A bathtub. Cold beer. Women. I pulled the Chivas out of the drawer and treated myself to a drink. I had to find the fifth man, and I had an idea. Normally I have no megalomaniacal tendencies, but now I saw only one way to make progress in this case.

I walked up Kaiserstrasse in the direction of the main railroad station. Except for a couple of whores with umbrellas on the corner, the block was deserted. A small but raucous bunch of Americans went into a brothel. The neon lights looked dim in the rain, and there was no clientele to lure into the strip joints. A police car drove by on its rounds. In front of the Rio stood a lumpy figure in a napa leather coat. He looked like he'd been standing there for a long time. He grabbed my sleeve. "Hey,

Mustafa—come see classy women. Great tits, great ass. Real classy! No lie. And real cheap." I crossed the street. A blonde informed me she'd do it tonight for just twenty. "See, buddy, it's like a going out of business sale."

Finally I reached Ellermann's Game and Sports Center. The poolroom was on the second floor. As a frequent visitor, I knew the assistant manager. The poolroom was as desolate as the street. Two Japanese were shooting. Two five-hundred-mark bills lay on the side table. I watched one of them sink the eight ball and pocket the bills. Without a word they renewed the bet and racked the balls for a new game. In the back, an elderly gentleman was practicing bank shots. The assistant manager stood by a window and watched the goings-on in the hot-sheet hotel across the street.

"Evening. What's happening?"

He clicked his tongue.

"She's been haggling over the price for half an hour."

Now both of us were watching. "All right! She's got the bills. Now she closes the curtains."

He turned.

"Quite an odd show, that. But in this filthy weather business is bad, and prices go down. Red-dot specials in the red-light district."

He slapped my shoulder. "Well, Isnogood, how about a game?"

I nodded, and he went to get the balls. Karate—this had been his nickname ever since he'd kicked in the face a patron who had been unwilling to pay—was a born-and-bred native of this part of town. After doing some time for auto theft and bodily injury, he had stayed clean and was on friendly terms with both cops and pimps. Both cops and pimps came to shoot pool at his place.

He returned and racked the balls. I took the first shot, and we alternated all the way to the eight ball. Both of us missed it three times. Then he triple-banked it elegantly into a pocket, noting, "Your left arm is like jelly."

"I had an accident."

He grinned. "And the doctor prescribed schnapps? You stink like a still."

I growled noncommittally, and we played another game. As he was lining up his shot, I asked him, "Do you know anybody who'd like to make a little money? Five hundred marks an hour."

He made his shot, straightened his back slowly. "And what would he have to do during that hour?"

"Stand watch in front of the offices of the Criminal Investigation Unit. And maybe crack a safe."

"The Crime Squad, eh? I see."

We continued our game. After a while, he said:

"If you're not feeling too good—my girlfriend is on vacation. You can come stay with me for a couple of days."

"I wasn't joking."

"That's even worse."

"I'm looking for a murderer—or an accomplice who has connections to the police. His name should be on a list of informers. At least, that's what I think. In any case, he must have turned in four alleged suspects in exchange for being let go, and he's probably under contract now. The detective superintendent in charge of the case is tremendously proud of these successful arrests, and I'm the last person to explain to him that he has released the only truly guilty party. On the contrary: He's busy weaving his web of informers, and he's worried that I might destroy it."

Karate sank the three.

"And you would like to clean out his office. How are you going to move those files and mountains of paper? In boxes, or in sacks? These days, or so I'm told, they have *archives*. So maybe you won't find anything at all in that office, and you'll have to get the archives and the computers too. I suppose it would be a good idea to call a cab to the front door."

He slammed the seven in, then scratched on the next shot, and it was my turn.

"I don't know anyone who'd do such a job without wanting to get paid in advance. And I don't even know anyone you paid in advance who would do the job."

I lit a cigarette and walked around the table, looking for a shot.

"Let's suppose the guy would have no trouble proving that I forced him to do it. As soon as we set foot in police headquarters, he should, in fact, persuade any questioner that I've arrested him without a warrant. If we get caught, that'll give me a chance to get away. I'll pretend I'm just a dumb private dick who's been trying to curry favor with the superintendent by this senseless arrest."

He pulled out a cigarette, rolled it morosely between his lips and growled, "A *dumb* dick? Not just dumb, totally out of his mind." He shook his head. "Listen, when you lose your license, I'll be glad to give you a job. Keep an eye on the place, shoot a little pool. Seven marks an hour. Nice quiet job."

6

The Dawn Restaurant. The Chinese lettering on the window was scratchy and flaking off. On the glass door, a pale green dragon blew smoke around the menu. Little bells rang as I entered. The booths were dimly lit by paper lanterns and decorated with dusty Chinese parasols. Disco pop was playing on the radio. The small Chinese man behind the counter was chewing on a toothpick and glancing at me with bored eyes.

"I'm looking for a Mr. Slibulsky."

He pointed his thumb at one of the dark corners. I ordered coffee and walked to the back, the top of my head grazing the colored paper garlands. Slibulsky sat at a bamboo table, drinking beer. The description fit. Short, black curls, puffy cheeks, unshaven, a drinker's nose. I sat down across from him.

"Ernst Slibulsky?"

He stared into his beer.

"Uh-huh."

"Kemal Kayankaya. Private investigator."

He drank his beer. Then he scrutinized me and said, "Aha."

"I'm told you're looking for work. I have a job for you."

My coffee arrived, and he ordered another beer.

"It pays five hundred marks an hour."

He leaned back, stretched his legs, and grinned. He commented that this would at long last allow him to hire a tax consultant.

"All you have to do is let me handcuff you and take you to the Criminal Investigation offices. Then you have to start carrying on and shouting that I had no right to do that."

"Shouting?"

"Only as we go in. If we manage to get out again, you better keep your mouth shut."

"And if we don't make it out again?"

"Then you go on playing the part, claiming you don't know anything about anything, saying I pulled a gun on you, told you I was a cop, and so on. They'll take no interest in you."

He told me I had a sense of humor and went back to contemplating his beer. I told him pretty much everything that had happened so far in the Böllig case. Not that I really trusted him, but it was my only chance to win him over. When I'd finished, he looked at me and asked, "Who gave you my name?"

I shook my head. I had given Karate my word. Slibulsky took a wooden match and stuck it between his teeth. Then he looked at me with a twinkle in his eye.

"And who won?"

"Come again?"

"I've never known anyone to visit Karate without shooting a game with him."

He pointed at my hands with his matchstick. "Blue poolroom chalk."

"We won one each."

He took out his wallet.

"Any friend of Karate's is all right by me. Even if he's a snooper, and is planning a really weird operation." He put twenty marks on the table.

"Make it eight hundred, and it's a deal."

I talked him down to seven. We paid up and left the Dawn.

"We'll go by my place first. Get a bit of disguise, handcuffs, and so on."

"And four hundred marks. The balance tomorrow."

Someone had stuck red fliers under the windshield wipers of all the cars parked in the street. "Jimmy's Jean Shop—Great Inaugural Hullabaloo!" I tossed mine into the gutter, and we drove off.

After pulling the brim of my hat down low over my eyes, I shoved Slibulsky into the entrance hall of police headquarters. The woman at the switchboard and the cop on duty looked up. I pushed Slibulsky straight to the reception window. As soon as we were in front of it and the woman slid the window open, he started ranting.

"Lemme go, you shithead, you goddamn snooper! I have nothing to do with any of it. Miss, he'll just tell you a bunch of garbage. He has no fucking right to drag me here. Or to beat me up either."

I punched him and leaned into the window.

"I have an appointment with Detective Superintendent Kessler. He'll be here any moment. If he should call from anywhere along the way, please tell him I've brought the man in."

She stared at me, dumbfounded. The cop came to the window.

"Do you know what time it is?"

"Listen, this is urgent. We may have to mount a major operation tonight ..."

"You're dreaming, snooper! I shit on your—"

"Shut up!"

Slibulsky played his part well. The two in the reception area were at a loss.

"All right, then? I'll wait for Mr. Kessler in his office. He gave me his keys."

I rattled my house keys.

"Oh well, all right." Then the cop grabbed his uniform

jacket and added, "I'll come along to make sure he does-n't give you any trouble."

I raised my hand.

"That won't be necessary. I can take care of him. Besides, no one's going to give me any grief later, if I have to use a little force. I'm not a policeman, you see," I looked at him with narrowed eyes, "but he has to sing."

He grinned.

"I understand. I'll notify Superintendent Kessler as soon as he gets here."

I nodded and guided Slibulsky to the hallway in which I seemed to remember Kessler had his office.

Behind my back, I heard the woman say, "But Mr. Kessler just ..."

"Let it be. It's gotta be something secret."

At last we stood in front of the door. I took out my skeleton key and worked on the lock. Five seconds later I had the door open.

"If someone shows up and there's time to get out, you knock on the door. If there isn't, you start playing your part."

"I hear you."

I closed the door quietly and switched on the light. The office was just as I remembered it. Only the silence was mildly unnerving. I sat down at the desk and went through the drawers. Typing paper, rubber stamps, the famous ruler, a city map of Frankfurt. At the very bottom, a pocket calendar. I took it. The skeleton key worked great on the metal cabinets. The first one was empty. The second contained coffee cups, aspirin, cookies, and shaving cream. The third, finally, held twenty-odd files. I went through them all. Was that a knock? No, I guessed not ... Then I read, "Investigation of Böllig case." Now there *was* a knock. Louder this time. Unmistakable. Slibulsky stuck his head inside and whispered, "You deaf? Hurry up, man!" I stuck the file under my arm, switched off the light, and shut the door behind me. The voices sounded quite close.

"What a mess! I was in the building. You saw me!"

Kessler! Slibulsky dragged me in the opposite direction. We had hardly reached the corner of the hallway before the light came on. We ran down the hall on our toes. Then the shouting began.

"They've broken into my cabinets! Don't just stand there, sound the alarm! They must still be in the building! Block all exits!"

We ran down a flight of stairs. No exit. I tried every door until one opened. The toilet. In the tiled wall at the end of the urinal gutter there was a frosted glass pane.

"That's our way out."

"How about taking these off me first?"

I unlocked the handcuffs. At that moment the siren began to wail. "Now we'll have some fun."

I took off my coat, wrapped it around my right arm, and smashed the glass pane. The frame was narrow, but we managed. Head first, I let myself drop the two meters down to the wet lawn. Slibulsky popped out behind me. We crawled over to some bushes. The building was brightly lit. A cop ran past us. The entrance had been closed. We had to cross about twenty meters of open space to reach the wall. Another cop appeared, gun in hand. Through the broken window we could hear them crashing into the toilet.

"They got out through here! Everybody outside! Shoot on sight!"

We had no choice. I held on tight to my file. "Now!"

We were up and running.

7

I had turned off the engine. I leaned back, enjoying my cigarette. It was a little past one o'clock in the morning. Lights were still on in The Dawn Restaurant across the street. Slibulsky sat next to me, quietly surveying the scene.

We sat there for a while, listening to the rain.

"Tell me: This job you're on—who are you working for?"

"The attorney."

"But he fired you! No, I meant generally. You're a private investigator. What a load of crap that must be."

He scratched his chin, ruminating. "The way you're going about it, at least. It's like—some kind of a cross between Robin Hood and a cop. That just can't work out too well."

"I have to eat. Ask a worker at the VW factory who he's slapping bumpers onto those cars for."

"But a VW worker would never risk his life to meet a delivery deadline. And he doesn't give a shit if the engine blows up after a hundred kilometers. Those guys back there were ready to *shoot* us. If we hadn't been lucky, we'd be lying there like a couple of dead rabbits in the grass. And who would give a fuck? Some little dealer from the railroad station, and a Turkish snooper. That doesn't even rate a mention on the morning news. They'd just plow us under in a hurry. So you risk your life for something you believe is justice, and end up in the compost heap. What's justice, anyway? It doesn't exist, not today, not tomorrow. And you won't bring it about, either. You're doing the same scheisswork as any cop. You catch the guys and bring them to court. You may be a little nicer, you may let one of them go, if you think he doesn't deserve a life behind bars. But you won't change a thing about the fact that it's always the same guys who do something, who get caught—not a thing, because the rules are set up that way. So all right, so tonight you pulled a fast one on the cops and you got away with a file. So what?"

The wind was driving the rain against the windshield. I watched the drops stream across it, running like a herd of hunted animals across the pane.

"I'm starving."

"There's an all-night place just around the corner where you can get hamburgers and breaded schnitzels."

"You want to go?"

"What about that fucking file?"

"Later."

I pushed the file under the seat, and we got out. We walked the hundred meters to the Schnitzel Fritz. It looked like a waiting room with fluorescent lights, green plastic tables, and chairs. Behind the counter a fat guy stood flipping burgers. The place was busy. There were some Turks, a couple of ladies of the night, and a table with giggling high-school kids gorging themselves on french fries and Cokes. We ordered schnitzels, potato salad, beers, and shots of schnapps. I had two shots and a beer in rapid succession. The schnitzel was cold, the potato salad drowned in vinegar.

"I work at my job because I wasn't able to go to law school. At first I thought that being a private investigator was a little bit like being a family doctor. Neither one can do anything about the great massacres and all the other shit that goes on all the time, but what he does do may be important to one individual or another. Once I had a killer explain to me that it was beneath his dignity to be caught by a dago, so he asked for a real cop to arrest him. Just before that I had offered him a shot of schnapps and told him that I would have preferred to send the other people involved to prison rather than him. Well, so. I've learned that it really doesn't matter one bit whether I exist or not. I do my work the best I can. That's all."

We kept ordering shots of schnapps to get rid of the aftertaste of our schnitzels. It started to grow dim, and I realized I wasn't all there anymore. The rounds kept coming, and I kept knocking them back. I didn't notice that Slibulsky was pouring his shots on the floor under the table. We attracted the attention of two high-heeled girls at a neighboring table. Their working days and nights had carved traces under their eyes. One of them got up and slid next to me on my chair, letting her leather miniskirt slide up over her thigh.

"Hello there, fellows—still up and about this late? Lonely in the night? Still up for fun and games, eh?"

She smiled, but her eyes were contemptuous. She lit a cigarette, scrutinized me through the smoke, and said provocatively, "I can tell that you could use a little loving." She ran her fingers through the hair on my neck. I closed my eyes.

"How about a visit to our little drawing room? It's just around the corner. A whole house full of pretty girls with wild ideas."

She shook my shoulder. "What do you say?"

I don't recall what happened after that. At some point, I regained consciousness and found myself walking arm in arm with the woman who told me her name was Fanny. We stopped in front of a building with a lot of red lights that blended into one Red Sea. I noticed Slibulsky, who must have been trotting along behind us. He grabbed my sleeve and I almost fell down, but Fanny helped me regain my balance. Slibulsky started saying things to me, and while he was talking, he was rummaging in my pockets. He pulled out my car keys and wallet, then spoke to Fanny and handed her a bill. I didn't understand any of it.

What did I care! Let him spend my money, let him toss the fucking file in a garbage can, let him drive my car into a wall! I was yelling at him. I said I hadn't asked him for any favors, and I told him to leave me alone, to mind his own fucking business. And anyway, this shithole of a world could go to hell for all I cared, and he with it. I was about to attack him when Fanny managed to drag me into the building. Men slunk past us on the staircase; a half-naked woman sat on a landing reading a newspaper. At last Fanny unlocked one of the green pressboard doors and dragged me to a bed with a blue silk cover. She lit a cigarette for me and took my clothes off. Then she sat down next to me and helped me take her clothes off, down to the last little bits, which she removed herself. I felt her skin against mine, naked and warm. My hands groped along her legs. Later I felt her moving above me, but all I saw was her breasts before I lost consciousness.

It was half-past four when I woke up and looked at my watch. My throat felt like a tanned piece of leather. It was still dark outside. Fanny lay beside me, asleep. I could see her face in the light cast by a street lamp. She had taken off her makeup. I could remember only half of the night, and would have preferred to forget even that part. I got up quietly, gathered my things, and put my clothes back on. I went to the window. The streets were still empty. Then I remembered the business with my keys and wallet. I cursed alcohol and Slibulsky and the whole world. If that file was gone ... I was an idiot. In a corner I found a carafe with water for my poor head. Fanny sighed in her sleep. I took her lipstick, wrote Thanks for Everything on the mirror, and mentally apologized for my quiet departure. I tiptoed down the stairs and through the plastic swinging doors out into the street. My watery knees took me in the direction of the Opel. A ragged creature on the curb was singing "Without you I can't go to sleep tonight," and tossing empty beer bottles into the street.

"Shut your face!" someone roared from the opposite building.

The old fellow pulled himself up with the aid of a parking meter, shook his fist, and yelled, "Come on down ... if you wanna knuckle sandwich, you ass-asshole!"

Then he slumped back and burst into sobs.

"What a shitty country ... an' shitty people ... an' nothin' to drink ... Shit, it's all sh-shit!" He lay down on his side and began to snore.

My Opel was still there, with a note on the windshield: "It's open." I opened the door and reached under the seat. The file was gone.

Dazed, I leaned against the car and stared at my surroundings. The rain had stopped. Then I saw that the light was on in the Chinese restaurant. This struck me as strange, and I walked over and tried the door. It was open. At the table closest to the door sat Slibulsky, bent over a stack of papers, a steaming cup of tea next to him. He growled, "There's coffee too, behind the counter. I bet it's still hot."

I helped myself to some and sat down at his table.

"Amazing what the cops manage to write about just a single case. This file is a gold mine. But what you're looking for isn't here." He pointed to the seat. "There's your wallet, and your keys. The shape you were in, you might've treated the whole bordello to champagne. I gave Fanny a hundred marks. That's less than the nightly rate; I don't know why, but she took you along for a hundred." He grinned. "Maybe she felt sorry for you."

"That's enough."

I forced myself to have some of the coffee. It tasted terrible.

"Who made this?"

Slibulsky clicked his tongue and pointed proudly to himself. "Original Viennese recipe. With a pinch of salt and a dash of genuine cocoa."

"I see." Then I lit a cigarette and examined the reports. The twenty-second of April was the date of the sabotage. I remembered Kessler's pocket calendar. I took it out, looked at it: Fourteen hundred hours, dentist; sixteen hundred hours, conference at G; sabotage at B. Chem.

On the twenty-sixth of April, when the four had been arrested, there was an entry that read: zero hours, operation Herbert K. In the back, where addresses were listed, I found an H. Kollek, Post Office Box 3278, Doppenburg. I grabbed Slibulsky's arm.

"I've got it!"

He cast a suspicious glance at the calendar, and after checking the entries, he murmured, "I've been sitting here since two o'clock, and ... Well, I'm not a family doctor." He grinned again.

I pocketed the calendar and got up.

"I have to go to Doppenburg right away."

"I'll go with you."

"Why?"

"You still owe me three hundred marks. I better stay with you, so you won't tell me later you spent it all boozing with some Herbert Kollek."

I picked up the file, and we left.

"Drive to the end of the street, then turn right, go once around the block. I'll be back down in ten minutes. If I'm not, you just take off."

"You really believe they've been waiting for you since two o'clock?"

"I don't know. Everything looks quiet. See you in a minute."

I got out of the car and walked the hundred meters back to my apartment. Listening by the door, I couldn't hear anything. I turned the key in the lock and stepped inside. Still nothing. By this time, Kessler and his boys would have pounced. I took off my coat, hung it on the rack, and switched on the light. Something smelled bad. I walked into the living room, switched the light on, and saw what it was.

Schmidi, unwashed, wearing yesterday's T-shirt, was reclining comfortably in a corner of my couch. Only the small dark hole in his forehead spoiled the idyll. I hurried to turn off the light and looked for my Beretta in the half-dark. It lay under the couch. Schmidi had been shot and killed with my gun. He had nothing on him, only his I.D. I took the I.D. and the Beretta, touched nothing else, and left the apartment.

Slibulsky drove up at a walking pace. I didn't waste a moment getting in. "There's a stiff with a hole in his forehead on my couch. Reiner Schmidi. The guy who beat me up yesterday."

"What did you do?"

"Nothing to be done there anymore."

We headed toward the freeway. By the railroad station, I asked him to stop. I dug out the address Nina Scheigel had given me.

"There's a Russian who lives around here who deals in contraband vodka. I owe someone a bottle."

Slibulsky stepped on the brake and complained. "You have nothing better to do, this godforsaken morning, than to cultivate your alcohol addiction?"

I told him there were always more important things to do, or else never, and a while later we rang the doorbell of Nikolai Herzel, Münchner Strasse sixty-three, third floor. It was a little before six. Wide awake and fully dressed, he came to the door. A small man in a black suit and brown fur slippers. I introduced myself and Slibulsky. I had hardly finished when he ushered us into the apartment. With a twinkle in his eye, he said in his raspy voice, "I know. Nina was just here. You missed her by minutes." He had to be past fifty, but there wasn't a single wrinkle in his face. He had a full head of very shiny hair. He seemed to be enjoying the best of health, and yet something didn't seem quite right. In the shabby living room furnished with decrepit armchairs and three television sets he asked us to have a seat. A teapot steamed on the kerosene stove. He crossed his arms and smiled at us.

"Well, gentlemen, to make a long story short, my current delivery is overdue, and my supplies are running low."

He paused deliberately, folded his hands, and continued:

"Such a situation is, naturally, reflected in the price."

He looked deep into my eyes.

"How much?"

He smiled and started pacing.

"Since it is Nina who sent you—let's say, a hundred and fifty for the half liter."

I glanced at Slibulsky who looked dumbfounded, then indicated that in his opinion, this little Russian no longer had both oars in the water.

"Let's get serious, comrade. We're just a pair of poor devils who want to give an old lady a present."

He demurred. "I know, I know, but what can I do? Times are hard."

"Eighty, and it's a deal."

His eyes narrowed.

"A hundred and forty. That should be satisfactory to all parties concerned."

Slibulsky rose and stood right in front of the little Russian.

"My friend and I don't see it that way. Only one of the fucking parties would be satisfied with a hundred and forty, and it ain't us. My friend is willing to offer ninety, and I'll go for a hundred, but that's it!"

He looked down.

"And when I say that's it, I mean it too. A couple of blocks from here, there's a guy who got his brain ventilated. And do you know why? Over the little matter of a case of cognac. So exercise your tiny brain now! All right, amigo?"

The little Russian looked scared. Cautiously he made his way past Slibulsky and out of the room. Slibulsky waved his hand as if to say, "Well, then."

We got our bottle for ninety and took off. Back in the car, Slibulsky said, "And I thought I was making money selling coke."

"Did you see the guy's skin? Smooth as a pool ball. And his hair."

Slibulsky cranked the engine.

"Arsenic."

"Come again?"

We were on our way.

"Arsenic, in small doses, is like a shot of whiskey before breakfast. If you manage to hold it down, you feel just great. If you take the stuff daily, your skin becomes smooth as a baby's ass, and your hair gets that buttery sheen."

"My goodness."

If it hadn't been raining again, we would have been driving into the sunrise. As things were, it only got a little lighter. We stopped for coffee at the first service area.

"When the cops find that dead comrade in your apartment, it's curtains for you."

I wagged my head.

"I think they already know he's there. But in the meantime, they also know that we got away with Kessler's files, and they're no longer so sure that it was such a great idea to add the stiff to my living room furniture. That was why they weren't there. They may be busy carting him off again."

I thought of all sorts of things. I took another look at Kessler's calendar and noticed certain entries that began last May and were repeated with weekly regularity. "Confer with M.!" According to the calendar, the last meeting had taken place last night.

"When do registration offices open?"

"No idea. Not in my field of competence. Maybe sometime between eight and nine?"

At eight o'clock, I went to the pay phone. Information gave me the number and I dialed it.

"Doppenburg registration office. Good morning."

"Möller, from the public prosecutor's office in Frankfurt. I'm working on the Böllig case. I need to know if a Herbert Kollek is registered in Doppenburg."

He sounded reluctant, but after I assured him that I would send him a written copy of my request, he went to check the record.

"Mr. Möller? I'm sorry, but you're too late. Herbert Kollek moved away from Doppenburg in nineteen sixty-nine."

"Where did he move?"

"To Frankfurt."

"I see. One more thing. That same year, sixty-nine, was the year Friedrich and Barbara Böllig's son was born. Unfortunately I can't remember his first name, but I'm told that he was institutionalized soon after his birth. Could you find the name of the institution?"

That took him ten minutes. A trucker was waiting for the pay phone, looking none too happy about it.

"The son's name is Oliver. He was born on November seventeenth, and is in the care of Dr. Gerhart Kliensmann, at the Ruhenbrunn Private Clinic."

"Thank you."

I hung up. Slibulsky sat at a table, grouchily perusing illustrated magazines. Without looking up, he said, "OK, you're the boss, you have the overview. But I sure would like to know what you think you're doing, calling registration offices."

I told him. We paid and drove on to Doppenburg.

▪DAY THREE▪

▪1▪

I pointed at Nina Scheigel's house.

"There it is, number seven. I assume he's asleep, he works all night. But just get him out of bed. If his wife is there, lock her up, tie her up, whatever. Act like a wild man, break something, but don't make so much noise you'll alert the neighbors. Tell him you know everything and want to be paid off, or else you'll call the cops. And as soon as he agrees to pay, make him tell the truth."

Slibulsky squinted at me. "What truth?"

"He knows something, but he hasn't been willing or able to talk about it. Who knows if it's the whole truth? But it may be a part."

"And if it isn't?"

"Then we're out of luck. Afterward, if you can manage it, call Anastas. Make it anonymous, but try to find out if the 'Freedom and Nature' group has been heard from again. You can do it."

He nodded.

"Sure. I'm an expert in making anonymous phone calls and beating up night watchmen."

I proffered the Beretta. He made a face.

"No thanks. Breaking and entering and bodily injury—OK, with a good lawyer; but I won't take the rap for knocking off Schmidi. Not for a paltry seven hundred marks."

"Suit yourself."

He shook his head, raised his index finger to his forehead. "See you later."

I headed toward the main drag. Half an hour later, I stood in front of the wrought-iron gate of Ruhenbrunn Private Clinic. The rain had stopped, and the large brick building looked peaceful in the morning light. Birds were twittering in the trees that surrounded the edifice, and white bedclothes had been hung out to air from some of its windows. A nurse was pushing a man in a wheelchair across the lawn. I pushed the bell. The intercom asked me what I wanted.

"It's a family matter. My uncle, well, he's really my wife's uncle ..."

"How's that?"

I stopped. The voice was aggressive. "Please express yourself clearly."

"Well, he's totally confused, and needs care."

"Why didn't you say so in the first place? For admissions, you need to speak to Mrs. Hengstenberger on the second floor, office number three."

The gate swung open, the sand squeaked under my shoes. The drive had just been raked, and I was the first to leave my footprints on the fine wavy lines. To my left, a large lawn extended all the way to the wall behind which Villa Böllig stood. A gardener was trimming rosebushes. Complete silence reigned. It almost seemed as if the clinic were closed until further notice. For a moment a head moved past a window, then a second and a third, until I realized it was just one person doing her rounds.

Near the entrance, I passed the patient in his wheelchair and his nurse. The patient giggled and said something. I walked through the glass door and up a flight of stairs. Then I almost collided with a mountain of flesh two meters tall. Dressed all in white, he looked like some kind of attendant or male nurse.

"Now, now," he said quietly. He was rolling a matchstick from one side of his mouth to the other. He stared at me with indifference.

"Sorry," I murmured. He smiled.

"I want to see Mrs. Hengstenberger."

He spat the match into a flowerpot and said, "Crazy, huh?"

When I said, "Not me, my uncle," he smiled again.

"Mrs. Hengstenberger?" I repeated.

He said, "Crazy, huh."

With a friendly nod, I pushed past him. He chortled. The door to office number three stood ajar. She was on the phone.

"... No, I'm sorry, the patient does not have permission to receive visitors ... not even his mother ... what was that? You got a letter from him? That's impossible, the patient does not have permission ... Nonsense. He's receiving the best medical care. No reason to worry, at all ... all right, I'll see what I can do. Good day."

She hung up and punched a two-digit number.

"Hengstenberger here. Kunze? Please check up on room thirty-four. He's managed to smuggle a letter to the outside. All right?"

I knocked.

"Come in."

It was a voice to cut glass with. Mrs. Hengstenberger was leaning over her desk, writing. An old book case stood in a corner, next to some health insurance calendar with flowers. The room was white and clean, with a view of the drive. She put her pen aside, folded her letter, and put it in an envelope. Without looking up, she asked, "How can I help you?"

"I would like to have permission to visit Oliver Böllig. He's been in your care for seventeen years."

"Your name?"

"Kayankaya."

Her face relaxed.

"You're not a relative? I'm afraid I can't give you that permission. I'm very sorry. Good day."

After a triumphant glance at me, she went back to the materials on her desk. I walked to the window and lit a cigarette.

"Smoking is not allowed here."

I bounded over to her. "Listen, sweetie"—she gasped for air—"I don't have a whole lot of time. I need that boy, or else the file on his illness and treatment. I need to know why he's been cooped up here for seventeen years. It's a question of a murder case. So just get me the file. Here ..."

I tossed my license on the desk. She picked it up as if it were dirt, glanced at it, put it back.

"I have to notify Dr. Kliensmann. Please wait outside."

I shut the door, sat down in the hallway. Everything was quiet. I lit another cigarette and shot smoke rings through the air. Now I could hear occasional cries, echoing as if from a great distance through the white hallways. I had just decided to go back in to get a little action out of Mrs. Hengstenberger when the mountain of flesh came up the stairs, a fresh matchstick in the corner of his mouth. He approached slowly and stood in front of me, his arms crossed. "Come with me," he said. Then he smiled, but his eyes remained cold. He led down a flight of stairs, then down another one. In the basement we walked down a hallway, until he ushered me into a windowless yellow room, lit by a fluorescent tube protected by a black iron grate. Thin rubber matting covered the walls and the floor. The mountain leaned against the door, still smiling. "Crazy, huh?"

I walked up to him with a twinkle in my eye. "Listen, you look like a smart fellow. Take me to your boss. If you do, I'll let you try out my car. On the freeway, if you like. OK?"

He looked offended, took a step forward, and punched me in the stomach. I fell down, and he said, "The doctor will be here in a minute." The door slammed shut. I reached for my loaded Beretta. Why hadn't I thought of it sooner? I crawled to the door, and an acrid smell rose into my nostrils. Something began to coat my brain like a layer of lead. In slow motion, I managed to pull the gun out of my pocket and aim at the lock on the door. "Sleep," I thought. "Sleep, and never wake up again." I almost forgot the Beretta while I pursued that thought, but the first shot woke me up. Then I emptied the whole clip into the door. My fingers clawed at the crack, and a moment later I fell through the door into fresh air. I dragged myself a couple of meters down the hall and sat down. Just as my head was beginning to clear again, I heard footsteps come downstairs, and the mountain of flesh reappeared with a pair of handcuffs in one hand. He looked at me in astonishment.

"How did you do that?"

I pulled the Beretta out from behind my back and let him take a good long look at it.

"Pretty good trick, eh?"

He looked offended, studied his shoes. Slowly, holding on to the wall, I managed to rise to my feet.

"Take me to the Böllig kid."

"Oh ..." He sounded scared. "The doctor won't like that at all."

I waved my cannon, and he led the way.

The Böllig kid was so tall he had to stoop if he wanted to stand up in his cell. I motioned to him to sit down again. With a dull gaze, he went back to his clothespin construction, his long back bent over the table. It seemed as if he had never learned to speak; he reacted to none of my questions. He was a seventeen-year-old wreck, nothing but pale skin and bones. A faint beam of light fell onto his worktable from a barred window. An iron bed stood in a corner. The mountain leaned against the wall. He looked miserable.

"How long has he been doing that shit?"

"Dunno. But," he came closer and whispered, "that's all they know how to do."

"But you, you know better things to do, don't you?"

Oliver Böllig could have grown up to be a big strong man, but seventeen years in Ruhenbrunn Private Clinic had turned him into an idiot beanstalk. He resembled his father, Friedrich Böllig, about as much as I resemble a Swedish tennis star. I stood there for a moment, watching the last of the Bölligs fiddling with his clothespins. I stood there a moment too long. Something exploded above my head.

"... an injection that paralyzes his memory. Kliensmann, I'll pay you whatever you want."

"That'll be expensive, madam. My reputation, my livelihood—you must understand. For less than five hundred thousand ... you see ... my silence ... and besides ..."

"That's all right. I'll get the money."

"But then there's something else too. You may remember. Until now you've refused, but today, I think ... You'll comply, won't you? Well, I too would have preferred pleasanter circumstances, but ..."

"What are you talking about?"

"Take off your clothes."

My nose itched. With difficulty, I managed to rub it against my shoulder. My arms were securely tied behind my back in a straitjacket that smelled of chlorine. I was lying in some kind of treatment room, and while I twisted and turned to loosen my bonds, the down payment for my blackout was being made next door. From time to time, Kliensmann uttered a few obscenities that made him sound like his own best patient. I crawled toward a picture framed behind glass. Slowly I slid up against the wall and managed to raise the bottom edge of the frame with the top of my head, until the picture came off its hook and crashed onto the floor between my feet. The two next door did not interrupt their activities. I started rubbing the straitjacket against the glass splinters that were still firmly lodged in the frame. Soon I had torn a small hole above my elbow. I kept working it against the splinter until it slowly cut through the jacket, my shirt, and my skin. I clenched my jaws and kept at it until a bloodstain spread over my right side, down to my waist. A little later I managed to extricate my arm. It looked as if someone had worked on it with a fretsaw. Now I was able to reach the leather straps on the back and open them. After wrapping a towel around my arm, I tiptoed to the door and listened.

"... We should do this more often."

No comment.

"So: five hundred thousand cash, within the next three weeks. If I don't get it by then, I'll go to the police. You understand."

"Three weeks? But I'll have to sell shares!"

"You'll manage. And the regular payments will continue, as usual."

Barbara Böllig used some foul language.

"Come on, take it easy. You're just buying some peace of mind. You'll *know* that snooper won't be able to make trouble anymore."

A door slammed shut. Barbara Böllig must have left. Kliensmann called Hengstenberger.

"I don't want to be disturbed for the next half hour."

I got into position behind the door. Kliensmann came in, halted, and I punched him in the jaw. While he was reeling across the room, I grabbed the tattered straitjacket and kicked him squarely in the ass so that he fell flat on his face. Then I wrapped him up in best institutional fashion, leaned him against the wall, and slapped his cheeks. Reluctantly he opened his eyes.

"Good morning. What was it you were going to shoot me up with, doctor? Just out of personal curiosity. I had dreams of going to medical school once."

"Bah!"

"Amazing, isn't it. Half a million down the drain. But it's nice to know one's value."

Kliensmann coughed and spat on the floor.

"That young Böllig ... I guess the charge would be clinical murder? What do you think?"

He turned his head away.

"In his seventeen years, has he ever seen anything but four walls and barred windows?"

Kliensmann remained silent.

"Why, do you think? Because he had the wrong father? Or was it the wrong mother? Interesting question. Or was it just because characters like you will do anything for money?"

"Bah!"

"You called Barbara Böllig as soon as you heard that someone was asking for her son?"

He didn't say anything. I got up and checked out the white medicine cabinet. I found some sleeping pills, got a glass of water, and hunkered down in front of him.

"All right, doc. Time to go beddy-bye."

He resisted. I had to slap him around a little before he opened his mouth; then I tossed a hefty dose of sleeping pills into his craw, poured some water on top of them, and held his jaws shut.

"That's it. Good night."

I left the room, locked the door from the outside, and pocketed the key. I found my Beretta in Kliensmann's desk drawer. I looked out the window at the leafless birch trees. My arms were throbbing. Now both of them were damaged. I wished I had a beer, I wished the fifth man were behind bars. Then I remembered Slibulsky.

■ **2** ■

The Roma was one of those Italo-German Frascati joints that demonstrate what cultural exchange is all about. Amid the oak paneling and furniture, the red-and-white checked tablecloths and fluted windows, the Pope in a gold frame looked just as good on the wall as the poster of the local bowling club. Juventus Turin shared a wall with the players of the Doppenburg team, and the pickled eggplant in the glass case tolerated a display of frankfurters right next to it. The flags of both countries were attached to a string stretched across the room. The place was empty, no waiters, no patrons. I found Slibulsky in a corner, between Bello Adriano and a mounted set of elk antlers. He was grumpily studying the menu.

"You must have had a great time. I've been sitting here for three hours."

I gave him a brief report. He looked at my arm and growled, "Have something to eat, my boy, and get your strength back."

I picked a mutton dish from the menu. No waiter appeared.

"Seems like this place is a little shorthanded."

"Once in a while you can see one pass."

Eventually a small, friendly Italian came to the table, and I ordered. Then I lit a cigarette and waited for Slibulsky to tell me about his morning. When he remained silent, I prodded him.

"What did the night watchman tell you?"

Slibulsky tongued his toothpick into a corner of his mouth.

"He didn't tell me anything. He wasn't even there."

The waiter brought two cups of coffee.

"This morning he left the house with some suitcases. That's what the baker across the street told me. Then he went to the airport. I heard that from the cabbie."

"He took a taxi?"

Slibulsky nodded.

"Paid with a five-hundred-mark bill."

"And his wife?"

"Left just a little later, went to the railroad station, and took the first train to Frankfurt."

"To buy her vodka. Is that all?"

Slibulsky gazed out the window.

"I talked to your lawyer. The 'Freedom and Nature'

people haven't called again." After a pause: "Why should they? Now that there's a warrant out for you, for murdering that guy."

"Schmidi?"

"Right. Murder, and robbery too. There's a police artist's sketch of your partner that looks quite a bit like me. I'll put it up on the wall between the Playmate and the barred window. If they allow pinups in the joint."

My mutton arrived.

"I could turn you in. Then I might stand a chance."

"Go ahead."

"It would be too tacky."

The waiter stood behind the counter, tuning the radio to the two o'clock news. The headlines were followed by a police announcement. They were looking for a Turk who spoke German without an accent and traveled in the company of a short man with curly dark hair. "... The suspects are thought to be in the Frankfurt or South Hesse area. You may call any ..."

"Let's get the check."

Slibulsky was getting into his overcoat when the waiter came over.

"Gentlemen, please. Enjoy your meal. Don't worry."

"He squeezed my hand.

"I'm from Naples. Beautiful city, beautiful people, but police," he made a fist, *"tutti figli di una putana!"*

We sat down again. The waiter wished us *guten Appetit* and went back to the counter. Slibulsky growled, "Let's do our next heist in Italy."

"For the murder, I've got an alibi," I said.

"You do?"

"Yes. It happened while we were breaking into the Criminal Investigation office."

"That's reassuring. So it's breaking and entering and grand larceny. Maybe they'll let us share a cell. You play chess?"

He looked out the window again.

Meyer stared at us. He was clutching the edge of his desk.

"You ... you what?"

"I need the personnel files on everybody who was employed here between nineteen sixty-seven and nineteen seventy."

Meyer risked a smile and stammered, "But, but the police were just here ... because of you. I ... I have to report ..."

He was fumbling for the phone. I pulled out the Beretta and put it on the windowsill.

"Call your personnel department. And no funny business."

At the sight of the cannon he turned white around the gills and did as he was told. After he had hung up, I asked him, "The cops were here?"

He gave a quick nod.

"What did they want?"

He looked at Slibulsky anxiously, then at me again.

"They want you, for murder ..."

He fell silent. Slibulsky stood leaning against the door, arms crossed over his chest, and growled something. I looked out the window at the refreshment stand run by

Friedrich Böllig's mother. Then the same fat guy appeared and heaved the files onto the desk. Ten minutes later I had it, black on white. Herbert Kollek, head of Böllig Chemicals' publicity department, had been summarily dismissed on the tenth of December nineteen sixty-nine. I pulled out the page and stuck it in my pocket.

"How long have you been working here, Mr. Meyer?"

He looked puzzled. "I started out in the warehouse, in fifty-eight."

"Did you know Herbert Kollek?"

"Yes ... Of course I did."

"Why was he fired?"

"Oh, you know ..." He swallowed. "I don't really ... What I mean is, Mr. Böllig must have had his private reasons. They'd known each other from their student days."

I went to the window and picked up the Beretta.

"They were friends?"

"I suppose ..."

He looked at the floor.

"And then one day they became enemies. Do you have any idea what Kollek is doing these days?"

He looked up, surprised.

"But don't you know—?"

"Yes, I know." I paused for a moment. "Now I do know."

I picked up length of sturdy string that had been used to tie the bundles of files. I went to Meyer.

"Put your hands behind your back. I'm sorry. But it'll all be over by tonight, at the latest."

Looking miserable, Meyer offered no resistance. I gagged him with my scarf. Slibulsky shook his head.

"Watch out this guy doesn't die of fright. If he does, that'll be another charge."

I set Meyer down on the floor. Slibulsky and I walked out and locked the door. The secretary was not in evidence.

The phone rang three times.

"Kessler here."

"Kessler? Did you know that Herbert Kollek has been able to combine his duties as your undercover agent with his own private interests in a truly remarkable manner? Have you never asked yourself why he keeps a post-office box in Doppenburg?"

I hung up.

A little later, I stood leaning against a tree and smoking a cigarette. Slibulsky complained about his wet feet and babbled about palm trees, beaches, and pretty girls. It was raining again. We were standing about five meters from the wall surrounding the Böllig villa. To our right we could see the factory smokestacks, to our left, the tops of the birch trees on the clinic grounds. All was quiet. The Mini and the Mercedes were parked in front of the door. The lights were on in the house.

I pulled a hip flask out of my back pocket. We sipped, smoked, and shivered. I decided to take another look at Kessler's calendar, and studied it for the next two hours. He had made careful and conscientious entries on every little thing, even including soccer games he was planning to attend. This didn't make for particularly exciting reading, but there were four short entries that cast a blinding light on the Böllig affair. In all four cases, they referred to a certain M.

May fifth: M. confidentially asks for help re: Rhein Main Farben, change public opinion.

May eighteenth: M. approves K. and Operation B. M. urges early date, suggests first week in June.

June sixth: K.'s operation group not ready to strike. New date: June twenty-second. M. agrees.

July twelfth: M. pleased with developments. K. paid off; possibly neutralize later.

Then it was show time. Two headlights bored their way through dusk and rain and up the drive. One person got out and disappeared in the house. Slibulsky spat.

"Let's go."

We climbed over the wall and dashed from one Christmas tree to the next toward the bungalow. The car had a Frankfurt license plate. I noticed something red stuck under the Mini's windshield wiper: "Jimmy's Jeans Shop—Great Inaugural Hullabaloo!" I motioned to Slibulsky to wait, and slid across flowerbeds to the glass wall of the living room. The big room was almost dark, lit only by light coming from the kitchen. I recognized the two men—a small one who was pacing around, his hands in his overcoat pockets, and a tall one who was leaning against a wall and smoking. Kessler and Henry. I ran around the corner and found the kitchen window ajar. Slowly I opened it a little wider, and eavesdropped.

"You've gotten me into some serious trouble, my dear man." Kessler's suave voice hid the edge of the guillotine blade. "Let's not even talk about the fact that your choice of the Böllig factory was decisively influenced by personal reasons. We could have managed that. We could even deal with the fact that you then decide to move into this house, so that you and the widow can show all the world how opportune Friedrich Böllig's demise is for you both. That wouldn't have been so bad—we had our four culprits. And young widows and their lovers are pretty commonplace."

Kessler took a deep breath. Then he hissed like a snake. "But neither one of those things can be tolerated when a third party enters the picture, a party who won't be bribed or intimidated, but stays on the ball. And he is a factor," he sighed, "that makes the whole thing a little too shaky."

For a moment I heard nothing but the ticking of the kitchen clock. Then Henry mumbled, "You don't have to worry about the dago. He's already in treatment, at Dr. Kliensmann's. An excellent physician, and a good friend."

Kessler's voice was still like a talking serpent's. "But I do have to worry! The dago, who you claim is under your excellent doctor's care, called me two hours ago to let me know where my agent Kollek has been hanging out for several months without letting me know about it. I thought that over, and then I got in my car and drove here. And what do you know, my hunch was right on target. Herbert Kollek is not at all where I thought he would be, he comes to the door of the Böllig house, all comfy in his bathrobe!"

Henry growled something incomprehensible. Kessler snarled. "And what about this Kliensmann? Who else knows about this business? Mrs. Böllig, the gardener, the cleaning lady? Maybe we'll read about it in the papers?"

"Only the night watchman."

"You reported that, and we took appropriate action. If I've been informed correctly, he got on a plane to Paraguay this morning."

Neither one of them said anything for a while. Then Kessler asked, in a suspiciously friendly tone, "Well. Does anyone, including the watchman, know about your connection to me? Or do they all believe that you killed Böllig for his wife and his money? It could have been your own idea to cover up the murder with a political act of terrorism."

Henry thought this was his chance to rehabilitate himself, and made a fatal move. While he was still swearing by all that was sacred, that no one knew anything about his link to Kessler, I broke into a run. Rounding a corner, I stumbled on a wire and crashed into a flowerbed. Rounding the second corner, I waved and whistled to Slibulsky, who didn't understand and just stood there, flapping his arms in the air. After the third corner, I pulled the Beretta and charged the front door. That was when the shot rang out. I stopped for a moment, crashed through the half-open door, and collided with the coatrack. I disentangled myself from a bunch of coats and sprinted into the living room.

Kessler, seated next to the telephone, gave me a quizzical look. Beside him, on the floor, lay Henry, the kitchen light reflected in his glazed eyes. His bathrobe had slid off his shoulders, and I could see the blood trickling from his chest down to his stomach. Kessler replaced the telephone receiver and got out of his chair.

"I found the fifth man. Regrettably, he resisted arrest and became violent, so I had to ..."

He made the appropriate gesture.

■ **4** ■

I looked him straight in the eye. "You won't get away with that, Kessler. I still have your fucking calendar."

He looked away.

"It's a deplorable business, you're right about that ..." He ran his palm across his forehead. "But that calendar won't do it, not in my case."

Suddenly Slibulsky appeared. He stood next to me and eyed the scene in bewilderment.

"Allow me—Detective Superintendent Kessler, this is Ernst—"

Slibulsky snapped, "Shut up! You want him to write me postcards?" Kessler smiled. I took the keys to Meyer's office out of my pocket and handed them to Slibulsky.

"Release that little guy. Tell him that he is Numero Uno at Böllig Chemicals until further notice. He'll enjoy that."

Slibulsky nodded and made tracks. I spotted a decent bottle of bourbon behind the house bar, poured myself a stiff drink, plopped myself on the couch, and encouraged Kessler to have a seat as well. He refused, stood there with his hands in his overcoat pockets, and asked me calmly,

"What are we waiting for?"

I put down my glass and lit a cigarette.

"I want to tell you something about Kollek."

"What if I'm not interested?"

"Then you'll listen to me anyway, or else I'll put you through the shredder!"

I put my feet up on the cocktail table and told him the story. Kessler pretended to be bored, cleaned his nails, sighed at regular intervals. But his eyes were wide awake.

"On November seventeenth, nineteen sixty-nine, nine months after her marriage to Friedrich Böllig, Barbara Böllig gives birth to a son, Oliver Böllig. How touching, one might think, the kid was conceived on their wedding night ... But on December tenth, almost a month later, Herbert Kollek, head of the firm's publicity department and an old college buddy of Friedrich's, is summarily dismissed from his job. A little later, he moves to Frankfurt.

Oliver Böllig, for his part, is transferred quite soon after his birth to the Ruhenbrunn Private Clinic run by a Dr. Kliensmann, where he is busy constructing things out of clothespins to this very day.

"I went to see the kid today. He doesn't particularly resemble his official father, as far as I can tell from photographs. And Kliensmann has been receiving, for many years, an excessively generous consultant's salary from the Böllig firm, without having to provide any tangible services."

"How nice for him."

Kessler smiled, back in his balloon-man mode.

"This is how I figure it all hangs together: Barbara Böllig cheated on her freshly caught factory owner on that same wedding night, and she did it with Kollek. After the kid was born, it became evident that Friedrich Böllig couldn't be his father, and it didn't take Friedrich long to find out whose offspring it really was. So he kicked Kollek out and made the infant disappear, not wanting a daily reminder of his cuckoldry. He must have paid off Kollek. Then he paid, and kept on paying, Kliensmann a lot of money to have the child put away as a retarded person in that loony bin next door. It was just a coincidence that I ran into Kollek on my first visit here, as Henry, the friend of the family. It was only today, after something the business manager said, that I realized that Kollek and Henry had to be one and the same. He and Barbara Böllig had kept up their relationship all these years, and you helped them solve the problem that Friedrich Böllig's continued existence was to them."

Kessler raised his eyebrows.

"I helped them?"

I lit my next cigarette.

"Kollek reached the goal he had pursued for seventeen years. He had the lady, he had the factory, he had made it."

I smiled at Kessler.

"And you thought, all the while, that he had killed Böllig for whatever you or your mysterious friend M. paid him to do it. Or that's what you thought until I called you this afternoon."

Kessler pricked up his ears at my mention of M. His eyes were tiny and alert.

"Not to belittle the results of your more or less," he coughed discreetly, "accurate research—but what does all that have to do with me?"

He got up and strode through the room. He stopped next to Henry's corpse and raised his index finger.

"All I'm concerned with is the fact that this man," he touched the corpse with the tip of his shoe, "is the fifth man we were looking for."

Like some petty criminal protesting his innocence, he spread out his arms. "I received a tip, and I drove here today. However, the suspect wanted to avoid arrest, and in order to prevent his escape I had to use my firearm. Unfortunately," he clapped his hands above his head in a gesture of regret, "I slipped on that rug, and so the bullet, unfortunately, did not strike him in the leg, but in the chest."

I looked at the corpse. "Unfortunately indeed. You plugged him right through the heart."

"Yes, well." He rubbed his hands and grinned provocatively. "That's my story."

Outside, night had fallen. I got up and switched on the light. Then I walked over to him.

"Maybe the magistrate would find your version quite acceptable. But—there is proof that Kollek was your undercover agent, not just some hoodlum you happened to shoot dead. Yesterday morning you were still bragging to me about your finely spun web of informers. Does it no longer exist?"

I stopped in front of him and looked into his eyes. He didn't flinch this time, and whispered, "That may well be true. But except for you and me, no one knows anything about it, and I am a German Detective Superintendent, and you, Kayankaya, are just a Turkish alcoholic with a private investigator's license. Don't you see?"

I whipped out the Beretta and pushed it into his stomach. With my left, I grabbed his collar. "Don't you see?"

Then I relieved him of his gun and let him go.

"You're lucky. I really would like to remodel your face, but I still have to take you to the public prosecutor's office. And La Böllig will come along too."

I turned. "Where is she, anyway? Her limo is right there in front of the door ..."

Kessler sat down and stretched his legs.

"Barbara Böllig has gone to a tea party. There's a note." He pointed at a shelf. I picked up the note and read it. "I'm at Scheigel's for tea. She has smelled a rat. I'll bring her to her senses. Later, BB."

I rushed to the phone, whipped out my notebook, and dialed Scheigel's number. No one answered. At that moment, Slibulsky toddled in and made a cheerful report. "That little guy was lying there, trembling like a fish. Boy, did he make tracks ... I've never seen anyone so happy ..."

"Shut up! Here!"

I tossed Kessler's gun at him. He caught it in surprise.

"Keep an eye on him! If he tries to get away, shoot him in the legs!"

I looked at Kessler pointedly. Slibulsky opened his mouth, shook his head, and watched me go. Halfway down the drive, I had an idea. I ran back into the house, ignored their amazement, and got the phone book. What was her maiden name again? Kasz ... Kasz ... Kaszmarek. Nina Kaszmarek, Am Südhang number five. I dialed the number. It was busy.

"Kessler, give me your car keys!"

He pursed his lips. "Do I have to?"

I took two long steps and punched him in the jaw, twice. He tumbled to the floor. His keys in hand, I repeated my instructions to Slibulsky and ran to his car. I sped down the drive, across the factory grounds, and down the main street into town. I stopped at a tavern and asked for directions to Südhang. They were given to me with typical South Hessian deliberation, and I jumped back into the car. Südhang was in the outskirts of town, one of the less successful housing developments of the sixties: Tall yellow buildings with one- to three-room apartments, surrounded by narrow strips of lawn and a tidy children's playground. There was a bicycle path, a picnic area shared by three buildings, an Edeka chain store, an ice-cream bar, a "Dogs Must Be Leashed" sign, and a wastebasket next to every lamp post.

I screeched to a halt in front of building number five, ran to the door, and slapped my palm on the buzzers. A faint voice came over the intercom.

"Who is it, please?"

"Public Emergency Force!"

"Oh my God my God!"

"A reactor at the Biblis nuclear power station is about to go critical in just a few minutes!"

"Oh, I see!"

I waited for her to buzz me in. Instead she asked me, "Should I close my windows?"

I roared that she should let me in, first of all, and then I charged up the stairs like a madman, knowing it was too late.

■ 5 ■

"What a surprise."

Nina Kaszmarek was wearing a black taffeta gown with a black lace collar, black high-heeled shoes, black silk stockings, and long black gloves. Her neck, arms, and ears were adorned with heavy gold jewelry. Her hair was carefully coiffed, her face was elegantly made up. Her eyes were shining; I couldn't tell whether this was from alcohol or tears. Perhaps both. She opened the door wide.

"Do come in, and don't mind my getup. This is my last evening here, so ... I'm packing my things."

I nodded and entered. She closed the door behind me and said, "Just come right in. I think I know why you're here."

The apartment was silent as a tomb. The small entrance hall was lit only by candlelight emanating from the main room. Two small doors led off the hall, probably to the kitchen and the bathroom. I entered the main room slowly. It was bigger than I had expected. Gigantic, overloaded bookshelves lined all four walls, interspersed only by the two windows. Twenty-odd candles, artfully distributed around the room, provided a warm yellow light. On a low table stood a magnificent steaming samovar, with two cups next to it. One of the cups was empty. The rest of the furnishings consisted of a small record player, records, a rocking chair, two heavy burgundy armchairs, and in the middle of the room, a white divan bed. One of Nina Scheigel's Russian cigarettes crackled quietly in a marble ashtray. On the bed lay Barbara Böllig, her hands folded over her midriff, staring at the ceiling. Candles to her right and left lit her face. It was a kind of wake.

"Quite a production."

I went to Barbara Böllig. Her hand was ice-cold. I turned and asked, with a glance at the samovar, "Arsenic?"

Nina Scheigel retrieved her cigarette and sat down in one of the armchairs.

"Are you always such a Sherlock?"

"No. But I paid a visit to your friend Nikolai this morning, soon after you had left. He must have supplied you with the stuff. But why today? Why not five months ago?"

"I caught Fred last night, with the money. He told me everything before he took off."

"How much did they pay him?"

"Fifty thousand. For going away forever."

Not a whole lot, I thought. I surveyed the bookshelves. "You sure had a lot to read here."

"How else do you think I could have passed the time?"

I lit a cigarette. "You're packing? Where are you going?"

"To the police."

I turned to her abruptly and shouted, "Why, goddamn it—why did you do it?"

She gulped. "The story had to have an end. And not just any end, but exactly this one."

She pointed across the room.

"This woman took Friedrich Böllig away from me. She did not let me come to his funeral. As I found out yesterday, she was an accomplice to his murder. All these years I have had to drown my thoughts and my grief in drink—and I should let her get away with all that scot free? I could not let that happen. This is my farewell party ... my farewell to it all! A little dramatic, but I like it that way."

She coughed.

"You'll go to prison."

She got up and walked to the window.

"You think this is better than a prison? It's a cave filled with bad memories. How many years do I have left? Who will find me?"

"Did you spend a lot of time here?"

"A couple of hours every day. I used to read, write letters to the dead. Whatever old people do to pass the time."

I brushed off this last with a wave of my hand. "What did Fred Scheigel tell you about the night of the murder?"

"They had fired him the day before. He was afraid to tell me, so he just went to his hut at the factory as always, but this time only to get drunk. When he heard the shots, he ran outside and found Friedrich. Dead. He must have sat there for a moment, because when he turned around, that Henry was standing behind him. Henry must have gotten rid of the gun. Otherwise, I'm sure, he would have shot Fred too. Then there was that explosion. Henry assured Fred that if he kept his mouth shut he would be given enough money to disappear from here forever. He only had to say that someone had knocked him down. Then Henry took off. A little later Barbara Böllig appeared, and when she too realized that Fred had seen something, she told him the same thing and promised him a lot of money."

She shrugged, sighed.

"Fred didn't particularly regret Friedrich Böllig's death. Besides, he was glad of the chance to get away from her at long last, with the money he was offered. And the detective accepted his story without questioning it."

"And the detective's name was Kessler?"

She nodded. I clapped my hands.

"Genius! The guy's a genius."

Nina Scheigel looked puzzled. I didn't go into that, but told her, "It was you, wasn't it, who killed Otto Böllig back then? With arsenic. You thought that would make everything all right with Friedrich."

She smiled.

"That's so long ago. Who cares about it now?"

She was right. Ultimately, I didn't give a damn. I paced back and forth and tried to clear my head.

"You've killed my only remaining witness. Henry's gone."

Once again she didn't understand, and once again I let it ride. I cast a glance at the corpse. "I brought you a bottle of vodka from Nikolai."

"You are a strange young man."

"Why did you do it?" I asked, myself more than her. Then I said, a little too loudly, "I have to take you along now."

She cleared her throat and asked, "May I ask you a favor?"

"Well?"

"Let me pack my suitcase and go to the police by myself. By myself, do you understand? I don't want to be taken there."

I nodded and walked to the door.

"You can run away, for all I care. It won't make any difference."

She laughed sadly.

"Where would I go? No, no. If you want to be nice to me, send the bottle to jail. There won't be a whole lot of difference between drinking it there or here."

I bit my lip.

"Farewell, Mrs. Kaszmarek."

" 'Well'? Don't poke fun at me, young man."

In the candlelight, her face was that of a painted old alley cat. Her green eyes were smiling.

I pulled the door shut behind me and walked slowly down the stairs. Halfway down, other ladies living in the building came rushing out to ask me what I knew about the Biblis disaster. I just walked past them. In the street I turned my face up to the rain. The cold droplets felt good.

■ 6 ■

As we stood outside the door of the Public Prosecutor's Office, I began to feel queasy. Kollek and Barbara Böllig were both dead, and if Kessler stuck to his story that he had had no idea about any of it, his calendar was my only piece of evidence. And that didn't seem like a whole lot.

Kessler knew this. He gave me a threatening smile.

"Kayankaya—mark my words, you'll regret beating me up."

"I only regret that I didn't snuff you."

Slibulsky had preferred to stay in the car. He said he had met enough magistrates to last him a lifetime.

It was almost ten o'clock at night. Lübars had been reluctant to come to his office at such a late hour. I knew him well, and he rather liked me, whatever that was worth. He was a public prosecutor, first and foremost. As soon as I mentioned Kessler to him on the phone, he regretted that he had agreed to come.

Finally he arrived, his hair none too well combed, and not wearing a necktie. He was of average height, bloated, and red-faced. He greeted us, briefcase in one hand, a bunch of keys in the other. "Good evening—good evening, Mr. Kessler. Please excuse my getup. But I thought I was done for the day ..."

Kessler laughed tolerantly.

"Right, right. I could think of more pleasant ways to spend an evening too, but ..."

He cast a withering glance at me. We entered Lübars's office. A handsome desk, two visitor's chairs. While I planted myself in one of them, Kessler said, "Tell me, Mr. Lübars, how is your wife? I heard she was ill?"

At the word "ill" he looked at me and showed his teeth.

"Thank you, thank you, she is doing better. Please be seated."

Kessler sat down in the chair facing me. Lübars slid behind his desk, put on his glasses, and folded his hands.

"I hope we can clear this up as quickly as possible. Both Mr. Kessler and I have had a strenuous day." They nodded to each other.

I asked myself how much influence Kessler had in the system. Perhaps it was due to his friendship with "M"?

"Now then, Mr. Kayankaya, when you called you said

that you would bring in a murder suspect." He coughed discreetly, glanced at Kessler. "But surely that was some kind of joke?"

Kessler said, with an impassive expression, "Sometimes my young colleague tends to hyperbole. It does get him into a lot of trouble." When he said "trouble," he wasn't looking at me, for a change, but at Lübars, whose smile was pained.

"Please tell me about your suspicions, Mr. Kayankaya." Then he mustered his courage and said to Kessler, "There's got to be something to it—otherwise you wouldn't have volunteered to come, Mr. Kessler."

The detective superintendent waved his hand in a gesture of magnanimity. He said, in a low, paternal voice, "I thought it would be best to get the matter cleared up once and for all, in the presence of a higher authority. So the young colleague can return to the firm ground of reality."

Lübars nodded and gave me a questioning look. I cleared my throat and tried to marshal my thoughts. I was in a lousy situation, and it didn't help that I knew it. Three hours ago I had been sitting pretty, holding a trump card: Kollek. Now I had nothing but trash cards, and it was time to lay them on the table. To stave off defeat, I decided to start out by bluffing. "Kessler, you've lost this game, and you know it. And I would like to ask you to kindly keep your mouth shut, and give Mr. Lübars a chance to listen to me in peace and quiet."

Kessler made an astonished face and looked at Lübars. "Do I have to—"

"Please, Mr. Kayankaya, let's hear it!"

Lübars was desperately moving things around on his desktop and avoiding both our eyes. The blotches on his face had turned a deeper red. I started my tale. I told him about Anastas, about the mysterious fifth man, the ice-cold widow, Schmidi, and so on, finishing with my theory of what had happened on the night of the murder.

Kessler sat in his chair looking cool, with a faint smile on his face, his head cocked to one side. Once in a while he scratched the back of his hand. Lübars seemed immersed in thought. Only his eyes kept darting glances at Kessler and me. Now he came to attention. "So you are saying that five people participated in the plot?"

"Six, to be exact. What alerted me at first were the statements given by one of the camping couple, the woman, and by old Mrs. Böllig, who runs the refreshment concession of the plant. Both of them said they had heard shots, and they confirmed that the shots were fired at Böllig *before* the explosion. Against these statements, we had Barbara Böllig's claim that her husband left the house only *after* the explosion. If one assumes that Kollek's accomplices had no interest in snuffing Böllig, and that it was impossible for Kollek to sprint back to the house just before the explosion in order to take Böllig out into the factory grounds and shoot him there, only one possibility remains: Barbara Böllig herself lured her husband out of the house on some pretext, and shot and killed him in a spot close to that pipe."

"If one assumes ... ," said Kessler.

Once again I told him to be quiet. Lübars took the ballpoint pen he'd been chewing on out of his mouth and asked, "Why would Barbara Böllig shoot her husband?"

I told the tale of Oliver Böllig, explained how long it had all been in the making. While I was doing so, I remembered that Kliensmann was still in that straitjacket in his office. Served him right. Finally I said, "There is a witness to my version. The night watchman saw a lot of it happen, and Barbara Böllig and Kollek bought his silence with fifty thousand marks. Which he is now spending in Paraguay."

With a glance at Kessler, I added, "As Superintendent Kessler informs me."

Kessler studied his fingernails and remarked casually, "Fred Scheigel was summoned to court as a witness. Since he wanted to leave the country, he had to ask for special permission. I just happened to hear about it."

"What if he decides he'd rather stay in Paraguay?"

"It's not my job to worry about that."

Lübars, wide awake now, adjusted his eyeglasses. After a moment's silence, he said, "All right. And where is this Barbara Böllig?"

Kessler looked triumphant.

"She is dead," I said.

The public prosecutor shuffled his feet under the desk and shook his head in disbelief. "Tell me more."

"She was poisoned. As we speak, the guilty party is turning herself in to the police authorities in Doppenburg. But that's another story. I'll save it for later."

Lübars shook his head again, but before he was able to respond, I went on to talk about Schmidi.

"Like the other conspirators, Schmidi believed that Kollek was a true comrade. Only after I pointed out to Schmidi how strange it was that the fifth man was still at large while his four buddies had been tracked down and arrested in only three days, he got suspicious. Obviously Schmidi had been a party to the plot, and he also knew how to get in touch with Kollek. He probably asked Kollek what was up, and Kollek had an idea. He realized that he had to get rid of Schmidi, and decided that the best place to do so would be in my apartment. Kessler must have told Kollek that I was trying to track him down. So he lured Schmidi to my place. Then, by a stroke of luck, he found my gun, shot and killed Schmidi with it, and was pleased with himself. Here's the gun."

I tossed my Beretta on the desk.

"The corpse is still sitting on my couch. A flyer that was distributed in Frankfurt that evening, stuck under the windshield wipers of Kollek's car, proves that he was in the city that night."

Carefully, with both hands, Lübars picked up the Beretta and looked at it as if it could whisper something into his ear.

Then he asked, "Fingerprints?"

"I'm sorry, but I still had a lot of errands to run, the kind where I look to have that thing on my person."

He closed his eyes as if all this were just too much for him, and put the gun aside.

"Don't tell me this Kollek is dead too. Or else why didn't you bring him along?"

"That's right. Kessler plugged him a little while ago."

Kessler raised his arms in regret and said in a tone of voice that mimicked remorse, "He was trying to avoid arrest. Unfortunately, I slipped on the rug. A stupid affair."

With a quick glance at Lübars, he added, "I'll probably be transferred."

"I see, I see," said the public prosecutor, not knowing what else to say. Then, when he found something: "It all sounds quite plausible. But how do you arrive at the accusation that Mr. Kessler has had an involvement with this matter that goes beyond his professional duty?"

I lit a cigarette and prepared Lübars for things to come by placing Kessler's calendar on his desk. It gave me courage.

"You remember the uproar about the Rhein Main Farben plant?"

Lübars looked irritated, as if I had been about to tell him a joke.

"Those were the people that sold mustard gas to Iraq, and soon after wanted to open a branch factory in Vogelsberg. Because of recent events, many people opposed the idea, and the Rhein Main Farben bosses had to come up with something to change what Kessler refers to as 'public opinion' in this nice little book. Nothing changes public opinion in this country more effectively than two sticks of dynamite, a murdered employer, and a grieving widow. Well, maybe the sad death of some dogs ... In any case, such a deed calls for revenge, and the best avenger is one who despite such tragic setbacks continues the lifework of the deceased. In this case, the field of chemical industry. So by all means, let's have the new factory in Vogelsberg. That was Kollek's and Kessler's plan.

"Kollek also saw this as a wonderful opportunity to take care of his private affairs with the Bölligs. His suggestion to make Friedrich Böllig the martyr was taken up with alacrity, since the firm is insignificant and has no major economic connections. So Kollek, with Kessler's assistance, recruited those four boys to set things in motion. But what Kollek didn't know—since he didn't have access to this little calendar of Kessler's—was that he too was slated for liquidation sooner or later. Tonight he was liquidated."

Without looking at either Kessler or Lübars, I picked up the calendar, opened it to the relevant page, and pushed it across the desk again.

"Kollek got paid for his part in the plot. I don't know where he and Kessler first met. Kollek came to Frankfurt in sixty-nine. He may have taken care of things for Kessler on previous occasions, or he may have been an effective informer. All I know is that they knew each other."

Then I tried to describe the conversation I had heard through the Böllig villa's kitchen window in as much detail as I could. Kessler was poker-faced. His eyes had become dark, narrow slits. Only his right index finger tapped quietly on the armrest of his chair. Lübars's hands shook as he picked up the calendar. Then he swallowed and said, "Who is M?"

I was able to help him. "Well, that's not too hard to figure out. The Mayor of Frankfurt is also the legal adviser to Rhein Main Farben. His wife owns a handsome packet of shares in that outfit. So M. stands for the Mayor. Kessler hasn't spent much effort on coding his notes here. The Mayor was the connection to Rhein Main Farben; he may have been the instigator of the whole thing. In any case, it was he who got Kessler started on the plot."

Slowly Lübars laid the calendar aside. He was clearly looking for a hole to hide in. He bent forward and said, with great effort,

"Mr. Kessler ... What do you have to say to that?"

For a while Kessler didn't say anything. Then he laughed for a while, sounding like a hysterical old woman. And then he stopped and said, quite calmly, "What could I have to say to that? It is incredible."

Lübars mumbled, "Yes, that's what I thought."

I stood up, furious. "Stop playing games! It's all in that fucking book! Or do you think the Superintendent just scribbled that in there for fun? What about Kollek's address?"

I pounded on the desk in front of Lübars.

"Why is it in there? Or can't I read? Or can't you read? Or can't anybody here read anything anymore? Tell me—

are those cooking recipes or love letters? Tell me!" I was roaring. "Yes, it is incredible, as you gentlemen just noted! But it is verified by this fucking page, in this fucking book, and this book happens to belong to this fucking superintendent, and it's his fucking incredible story ... But is it my fault that it's incredible?"

I rounded on Kessler. "And if you keep on staring at me like that, like some overstuffed carp, I'll punch your nose through your head so it leaves a hole for the daylight to shine through!"

Then I picked up the next handy object, a full ashtray, and threw it against the wall. After that I sat down.

For at least two minutes the only sounds in the room were my heavy breathing and Lübars's quiet cough. Someone said, "Mr. Kessler?" someone answered, "Yes." I didn't give a damn. I had done my bit, let them sort it out. I closed my eyes and thought about mild summer evenings in the grass, champagne in my head, and a flock of nut-brown girls in heaven. In the meantime, Kessler presented his version. The notes concerning M related to private matters, and Kollek's address had come to his notice in the course of the investigation. After all, he too had been looking for the fifth man. And Lübars said, "Aha, I see."

I opened my eyes when I felt a hand on my shoulder. It was Lübars's.

"Mr. Kayankaya, I must ask you to tell me the name of the suspect in the murder of Barbara Böllig."

I took my time lighting a cigarette.

"And if I don't?"

"Please don't damage your position any more than you already have. Otherwise I'll have to arrest you as an accessory to murder."

I stood up and let the smoke trickle slowly through my lips. I pointed my cigarette at Kessler, who was about to put on his overcoat.

"And what about him?"

Lübars took a deep breath that made his nostrils flutter.

"Mr. Kayankaya, I must warn you to keep such bizarre accusations to yourself in the future. I do not know how you arrived at such incredible conclusions, but I advise you to concentrate on a correct chain of evidence when you deal with another case. Mr. Kessler has been kind enough to refrain from a libel action."

The tip of his tongue briefly touched his upper lip.

"Do you understand me?"

I felt petrified. Only when Kessler wanted to pick up his calendar, I bounded to the desk and grabbed it before he could get to it. Fists on hips, he snapped at me, "My calendar, please. You won't get a chance to steal it a second time."

Without undue haste, I pocketed the little book. He came at me, tried to grab me. I rubbed my chin. "If you touch me, I'll beat you to a pulp."

He desisted. Lübars closed his eyes. Kessler said, "I must ask you not to leave town during the next couple of weeks. Your theory about the murder of this Schmidi does not sound convincing. It happened in your apartment, with your gun, and you did not notify the police. I am the superintendent in charge, and I will investigate your statement carefully. My calendar, please. Or," he cast a reproachful glance at Lübars, "would you prefer to stay here? I have all kinds of things on you, and the only reason I'm letting you go is to give you a chance to come to your senses and forget about your crazy story."

It was true, he could have nailed me. But he didn't

want to. He wanted to attract as little public attention as possible. I didn't feel like spending a night in a cell. I tossed the calendar on the floor in front of his feet. And that was that.

Leaning against the desk, I murmured to myself, "Great, Kayankaya."

Long after Kessler had left with an ironic salute, I was still standing there. Lübars went to his desk, shuffled some papers, and finally said, "I am sorry, Mr. Kayankaya." After he had let those weighty words sink in, he went on, "It may well be that your story was close to the truth—but you see, the Mayor ... A couple of ambiguous entries ... that's not enough ... And with such an accusation, I would be putting my head on the chopping block." He sighed, and repeated, "I am truly sorry."

I contemplated my shoes. "Why are you so afraid of Kessler?"

He picked up his briefcase, and we left the office.

"Well, he has a lot of influence, and ..." He locked the door, turned, looked at the floor. "It is well known that he and the Mayor are very close."

■7■

Slibulsky was trying really hard to be nice. We drove through the dark streets, raindrops dancing in the headlight beams. Small bolts of lightning flashed above the rooftops.

Slibulsky said, "Make a wish, I'll make it happen."

I thought for a minute while we were driving around a building site.

"I'd like Whitney Houston to sing for me. With just the two of us in the room."

I really meant it.

"Who is that?"

I put out my cigarette, leaned back, and said, "Oh, never mind."

When we stopped at the next streetlight, Slibulsky asked, "Where the hell are we going?"

"I dunno. Let's just drive around a little longer."

For a long while, neither one of us said anything. The engine hummed reassuringly. I pulled the bottle of Russian vodka from under the seat.

"Can you send things like this to someone in jail?"

Slibulsky looked doubtful. I pushed the bottle back and looked out the window.

"You know, I know this little bar, it's really a nice joint, soft music and so on ..."

I shook my head. "No, what I need now is *loud* music, well-rounded girls, and my head so full of beer that you can hear it sloshing around. Let's go to Sachsenhausen."

Slibulsky turned around, and we drove to Sachsenhausen.

Just as we entered the tavern, which, like all Hessian taverns, had an incomprehensible name, all the lights went out. We pushed through a chaos of lighters, candles, and howling patrons, and found seats at a table occupied by young men in their twenties. They were telling each other manly little jokes and downing quantities of hard cider. One of them had packed it in. He was resting his head on the tabletop and snoring intermittently.

After we had waited long enough, I got up and collared a waiter. He screwed up his eyes.

"Twelve beers? Just for you?"

"There's two of us."

"I see," he said, and I went back to Slibulsky. A little later the waiter wound his way through the rows of tables with a huge tray, unloaded it in front of us, and wished us good luck.

Behind me, some guy was slapping the table and shouting, "Hey, you guys, just think what it would be like to have a woman made out of beer. Just imagine! She'd be something! Just imagine!"

He sighed, and slumped against his neighbor's shoulder.

Slibulsky and I limited our exchanges to remarks like "Not bad, this beer," "Right, not bad at all."

The youngsters next to us were now busy scanning the hall for something to, as they put it, "slide over." A thin guy with bad teeth and short sweaty hair slapped my shoulder. "Look at that, buddy, that one over there! What a piece! Look at her boobs!"

The one right next to me roared, "Hey, Charlie, that's a Turk you're talking to! Turks only like women with huge asses. No head, no legs, just an ass, you know? This big ..."

I told the thin guy to take his paws off me, and asked the other one to step outside. He was a sturdy type with a square jaw and blond curly hair. His gaudy shirt was unbuttoned down to his crotch. The other boys looked at him expectantly. He got up slowly, and when two others wanted to follow his example, he waved them off. "I'll take care of this."

I asked Slibulsky to take care of the check. We wouldn't be coming back.

Once we were outside the door, the blond wasn't quite sure what was supposed to happen next. I took advantage of that, and quickly punched him on that square jaw, hard enough to take care of things. He staggered, fell down, and didn't get up. Slibulsky appeared soon after, and we marched to the car. I was tired. We drove off, and I started to snore after the first hundred meters.

A police siren woke me up as we were passing the main railroad station, and I asked Slibulsky to stop. I managed to get out of the car, reeled into the Traveler's Shop, bought a bottle of Chivas, and reeled back. Slibulsky eyed the whisky morosely and opined, "You don't give up easily, do you?"

I shook my head and went back to sleep.

Finally we stood in front of my building. Slibulsky leaned forward in the driver's seat. His voice was low and hoarse. "You're a pretty good guy, Kayankaya."

"Un-hunh," I agreed, and got out. He drove off. I tottered through the rain toward the front door, holding the Chivas with both hands. Suddenly a shadow detached itself from the wall.

"I've been looking for you all day. Two hours ago, Detective Superintendent Kessler himself called the editorial office to let us know that the four suspects are more or less innocent. The fifth man, someone named Kollek, had just been using the four to trick the police. Can you imagine?"

Carla Reedermann waved her hands excitedly, then looked at me with compassion. "I'm so sorry for you. You tried so hard. And the idea about the informer wasn't so bad, but ... Anyway, I came to tell you this so you wouldn't have to read it in the papers. And Anastas wants to apologize. He admits that he was a little ... grumpy yesterday." She smiled winsomely.

First I grinned, then I laughed out loud, laughed like an idiot, unable to stop.

"I don't understand ..."

"Never mind, sweetie. You understand lots of other things."

She looked confused, took a turn on the pavement, then said quietly, "The only thing I can't figure out is, who attacked Anastas?"

I tried to light a cigarette, but the rain kept extinguishing it, so I stopped trying.

"Well, Kollek, for instance, maybe together with Kessler, or with the Mayor, or with me ... or was it our Father in Heaven?"

Her hair and her overcoat were soaking wet. It was a pleasant sight, even when she got furious. "What is it you want? First you act as if you didn't give a shit, then you act like a wild man who won't give up on the case, and now you don't give a shit again."

I raised my arms.

"What do I want? I want some beer. More beer! Much more beer!"

Then I pushed past her and staggered down the sidewalk. Halfway to the door she caught up with me, said, "I'm sorry," and asked me if she could come up to my place.

I thought it over for a moment.

"There's a dead guy up there. Not a pretty sight. Maybe some other time ... Not now, I don't think."

I left her standing in the rain.

Then I was in my apartment. I wrapped Schmidi in two old bedsheets and dragged him out onto the landing. I poured myself a glass of Chivas and leaned against the window. A cat screeched, and down in the street someone shouted, "Red Front!"

I stood there for a while and stared at the rain.

January 1987

REAGAN CALLS FOR FINAL SOLUTION
OF PALESTINIAN QUESTION

GADDHAFI WORE JEANS!

Theo Sontag's political commentary: Was this a trick?

LEAK IN BIBLIS NUCLEAR REACTOR

The Minister of the Interior says, "Radiation negligible, no cause for concern among local population" and warns against "unfounded panic mongering."

U.S. DEFENSE SECRETARY ADDRESSES NATO

"We want a second-strike capability that renders a third strike impossible."

"BUT OUR WOMEN ARE MORE HONEST"

The Federal Chancellor in Bangkok at the end of his Asian tour.

FORMER MAYOR OF FRANKFURT
DECLARES HIMSELF WILLING
TO RUN FOR PRESIDENT OF
FEDERAL REPUBLIC

VERDICT AS EXPECTED IN BÖLLIG CASE

The four accused were sentenced to two years' imprisonment without probation. Many questions on the role played by Herbert Kollek remain unanswered. In his summation, the Public Prosecutor again stressed "the basic attitude of hostility against the state" of the accused.

In the eighty-ninth minute of the game, the Stuttgart team scored a regrettable goal and caused Gladbach to lose 2–1.

I put the newspaper away and dropped two aspirins into the glass. It was Saturday, ten o'clock in the morning. Outside it was snowing like hell. Next to my cup of coffee lay two letters, one from the Public Prosecutor's office, one from the Preungesheim Prison administration. I tore open the one from the prosecutor and read my third summons to be interviewed in the Schmidi case. Kessler kept on working hard to get me put away for murder. The one from the prison I held in my hand for a while. Then I opened it carefully. I was informed that Nina Scheigel, née Kaszmarek, had died in the night between the second and third of January. According to her wishes, I was being notified of the event.

I drank my aspirin, lit a cigarette, and sat there smoking until the phone rang. It was Slibulsky.

"Two o'clock, at Karate's?"

Sure, I said, and hung up. Then I made some fresh coffee.